FAMOUS REGIMENTS

The Black Watch

Other titles in this series

FAMOUS REGIMENTS

EDITED BY

LT.-GENERAL SIR BRIAN HORROCKS

The Black Watch

(*Royal Highland Regiment*)

(The 42nd Regiment of Foot)

BY

PHILIP HOWARD

HAMISH HAMILTON

LONDON

First published in Great Britain 1968
by Hamish Hamilton Ltd
90 Great Russell Street London W.C.1
Copyright © 1968 by Philip Howard
Introduction Copyright © 1968 by Lt.-General Sir Brian Horrocks
241 01538 3

Printed in Great Britain
by Ebenezer Baylis and Son, Limited
The Trinity Press, Worcester, and London

INTRODUCTION TO THE SERIES

by

LT.-GENERAL SIR BRIAN HORROCKS

IT IS ALWAYS sad when old friends depart. In the last few years many famous old regiments have disappeared, merged into larger formations.

I suppose this is inevitable; strategy and tactics are always changing, forcing the structure of the Army to change too. But the memories of the past still linger in minds now trained to great technical proficiency and surrounded by sophisticated equipment. Nevertheless the disappearance of these well-known names as separate units marks the end of a military epoch; but we must never forget that, throughout the years, each of these regiments has carved for itself a special niche in British History. The qualities of the British character, both good and bad, which helped England to her important position in the world can be seen at work in the regiments of the old Army. To see why these regiments succeeded under Marlborough and Wellington yet failed in the American War of Independence should help us in assessing the past.

Though many Battle Honours were won during historic campaigns, the greatest contribution which our Regiments have made to the British Empire is rarely mentioned: this has surely been the protection they have afforded to those indomitable British merchants, who in search of fresh markets spread our influence all over the world. For some of these this involved spending many years in stinking garrisons overseas where their casualties from disease were often far greater than those suffered on active service.

The main strength of our military system has always lain

in the fact that regimental roots were planted deep into the British countryside in the shape of the Territorial Army whose battalions are also subject to the cold winds of change. This ensured the closest possible link between civilian and military worlds, and built up a unique County and family *esprit de corps* which exists in no other Army in the world. A Cockney regiment, a West Country regiment and a Highland regiment differed from each other greatly, though they fought side by side in scores of battles. In spite of miserable conditions and savage discipline, a man often felt he belonged within the regiment—he shared the background and the hopes of his fellows. That was a great comfort for a soldier. Many times, at Old Comrades' gatherings, some old soldier has come up to me and said, referring to one of the World Wars, 'They were good times, sir, weren't they?'

They were not good times at all. They were horrible times; but what these men remember and now miss was the comradeship and *esprit de corps* of the old regular regiments. These regiments, which bound men together and helped them through the pain and fear of war, deserve to be recalled.

Regimental histories are usually terribly dull, as the authors are forced to record the smallest operation and include as many names as possible. In this series we have something new. Freed from the tyranny of minute detail, the authors have sought to capture that subtle quarry, the regimental spirit. The history of each regiment is a story of a type of British life now fading away. These stories illuminate the past, and should help us to think more clearly about the military future.

THE BLACK WATCH

A Special Introduction

by

LT.-GENERAL SIR BRIAN HORROCKS

IN 1923 THE Company which I commanded in The
Middlesex Regiment was attached to the Black Watch in
Silesia. We were part of a British Force sent there to
ensure that the plebiscite on the German–Polish frontier
passed off peacefully.

With typical Highland hospitality they went out of
their way to make us 'Cockneys' feel at home. I enjoyed
my time in the Black Watch Officers' Mess and was
even taught Highland Dancing, which is easier to perform skilfully wearing a kilt than in tight mess overalls.
I wonder how many people are alive today who can
recall 'The Lublinitz Lancers' as we called our equine
activities.

All regiments develop their own *esprit de corps* but it was
impossible to live with the Black Watch and not realize
that every officer and man whether Highlander or Lowlander belonged to one family, or rather to one clan, and in
the Author's words 'the clan pride of The Black Watch is
still handed down as a form of spiritual inheritance'. And
rightly so, for they have much to be proud of. They are the
original Highland Regiment. Their immediate ancestors
had been formed in 1624 when the Government started
raising independent companies of Highlanders 'to watch
upon the braes', while their record of hard fighting all

over the world must be almost unique in the annals of War. From Ticonderoga in 1758 to the battle of the Hook in Korea, over and over again, the 42nd whether called Black Watch or Highland Regiment have achieved the well nigh impossible, and when one reads of their appalling casualties—the 9th Black Watch lost 701 in one day during the Battle of Loos in 1915—it is no wonder that the Highlands are becoming depopulated.

What makes the history of this Regiment particularly interesting is that the clan spirit instead of making for uniformity, seems to have encouraged a rugged individualism which has often bordered on eccentricity, as witness Howard's account of how during the Reichswald battle when the 51st Highland Division was in my Corps, 'A Major of the 5th Black Watch was noticed walking down the middle of the street which was hissing with bullets, carrying an umbrella over his head. Presumably he had removed it from one of the houses. When asked why, he replied that it was raining. So it was, but nobody else had noticed.'

The 1st, 5th and 7th Black Watch formed part of the resuscitated 51st Highland Division, and we were together off and on from Alamein to the end in Africa, then again in Europe right up to the German surrender at Bremerhaven.

On the evening of the 23rd of March 1945, I climbed into an observation post overlooking the Rhine, on my Corps front. At 4 minutes past 9 I received the message for which I had been waiting—in its way an historical message. The Black Watch had landed safely on the far bank. So, the Red Hackles had done it again, for they were the first British Troops to cross and once more their old Regimental boast had proved correct. 'The Black Watch of the Battles': first to come (in the attack) and last to go (in the retreat).

Since 1961, Perth and the surrounding counties of Fife

and Angus must be sadder and duller places because these Red Hackles of whom they were so justly proud have moved their Regimental Depot to Aberdeen away from its old home in the Queens Barracks of Perth.

Chapter 1

IT WAS A time of war, and rumours of war; of civil war, of cold war likely to turn hot. Crowned heads rested uneasy. It all started, appropriately enough, in Perthshire—in the heart of the Highlands, the birth-place of valour, the country of worth.

The Highlands these days mean coach-loads of trippers roaring up the Sma' Glen, leaving a wake of potato crisp packets behind them. They mean tartan tourist trinketry, and purple Christmas calendars, ski-lifts and grouse moors. There is little menace and not much mystery left in the heather hills in the twentieth century. Well, it wasn't like that 300 years ago. There were no roads worth calling roads north of the Highland line. It took three weeks to gallop from London to Perthshire on a fast horse. And up in those scowling glens, the clans lived in a glorious tribal twilight, feuding and murdering their neighbours with monotonous regularity.

Soft southern citizens looked north over their shoulders with apprehension. A well-educated Londoner seriously asked in a letter whether the Highlanders did not kill their prisoners and suck their blood 'after the manner of other savages'. Any day a horde of hairy Highlanders, kerns and galloglasses, and quite possibly bloody thanes too, like something out of Macbeth, might come sweeping down from the ridges in a hurricane of steel. It happened in 1715, when the clans rose in support of James Stewart, the Old Pretender, poor old Mr. James Misfortunate. That time the bloody Highland blade was blunted at the Sheriffmuir.

But they might come again any day now—perhaps in 1745, to pick a date at random, for the sake of argument.

The original ancestors of the Black Watch appear upon this feudal scene in 1624. In that year the Government started raising Independent Companies, consisting solely of Highlanders, to police their wild homeland. Then on August 3, 1667, King Charles II issued a commission under the Great Seal to the Earl of Atholl to raise as many men as he thought necessary 'to be a constant guard for securing the peace of the Highlands'; and 'to *watch* upon the braes'.

This Highland Watch was supposed to prevent 'the lifting of creachs'—creachs mean booty, usually cattle. It was also to stop *Blackmail*, the original protection racket, by which the Highland freebooters extracted tribute from the plump, douce Lowland farmers. They were a rural police, against what their commission sternly calls 'thieves and broken men'. Various strongholds were appointed for the incarceration of 'drivers of creachs', and other nuisances. For instance the prison in Perthshire was the castle called the Blair of Atholl.

For the rest of the century these experiments in arming Independent Companies of loyal Highlanders continued. The experiments were not an unqualified success. At times the arms were used indiscriminately. The loyalty of the Highlanders was not always as unwavering as the Pole Star. There was a certain amount of corruption and fiddling on the side. Instead of bringing criminals to justice, the Highland Watch often 'compounded for the theft, and for a sum of money set them at liberty'. A General of the period reports that they also defrauded the Government by drawing pay for twice as many men as they had in arms. The accounts of one of the Highland Companies in 1678 show a certain amount of bold optimism in arithmetic as well as in spelling: 'Item, for 300 baggonets for the 300 fyrelocks at 2s stg. per peice—£360'.

In 1717, in the political turmoil and turbulence left by the 'Fifteen', George I disbanded the Independent Companies. A stern law forbade Highlanders to carry arms. Any clansman found with a claymore in his hand could be shipped overseas to serve the King in a red coat. An Edinburgh civil servant of the times explains that the Highlanders, 'being accustomed to the use of arms, and inured to hard living, are dangerous to the public peace; and must continue so until, being deprived of Arms for some years, they forget the use of them'.

Then in 1724 an Irishman, General George Wade, was appointed Commander-in-Chief in Scotland. He built the roads and bridges which gradually led to the 'civilization' of the Highlands, riding around on his surveys in the first English coach seen north of Edinburgh. The locals invariably took their bonnets off to the driver of the coach, 'as supposing him the greatest personage connected with it'. The pop song of the period ran: 'Had you seen those roads before they were made, You'd have lifted up your hands and blessed General Wade'.

Wade re-formed six Independent Companies of Highlanders reckoned to be loyal to the Government. They alone were allowed to carry arms. And their job, as before, was to police the Highlands, to keep order among the cantankerous clans. The 500 officers and men came from loyal Whig clans—three companies of Campbells, and one each of Grants, Munros, and Frasers. A private was paid 8d. a day; a piper 1s.

On May 15, 1725, Wade sent this order out around the glens: 'To Officers commanding Highland Companies— That pursuant to their beating order they proceed forthwith to raise their non-commissioned officers and soldiers, and no man to be listed under size of 5 foot 6 inches. That officers commanding companies take care to provide a plaid clothing and bonnet in the Highland dress for the non-commissioned officers and soldiers belonging to their

13

companies, the plaid of each company to be as near as they can of the same sort or colour; that besides the plaid clothing, to be furnished every two years, each soldier is to receive from his captain a pair of brogues every six weeks, a pair of stockings every three months, a shirt and cravat every six months'.

Pretty casual about the colour of the kilt, the Irishman seems to have been—'. . . as near as they can of the same sort or colour'. The meticulous R.S.M. on Adjutant's parade these days would burst a blood vessel if this original order were obeyed. Gradually the Black Watch tartan of the dark blue, black, and green sett came to be generally used. It became recognized as the 'Government' tartan.

The first official picture of the uniform of the Black Watch—1742.

14

While today the old dark tartan is worn around the world by civilians who have never heard of the Black Watch.

The dark tartan is supposed to have given the Regiment its name. The locals started calling the Independent Companies *Am Freiceadan Dubh*—the Black Watch. The Black comes from the tartan they wore, and the Watch from the watchful gendarme's eye they kept on the Highlands. Regular Guardsmen who were stationed in the Highlands had just started wearing red. The regular soldiers were called *Saighdearan Dearg*, 'red soldiers'. For instance, a Gaelic poem about the massacre of Glencoe written about this date runs roughly, being translated: 'Had we been under arms ere the hunt convened in the land, the folk of the Red Soldiers had returned no more to the host of the King'. The dark clothes of the Watch looked black beside the red coats of the regulars. At least, that is how the tale runs. This is not an entirely convincing explanation. The tartan, when all is said and done, is not black. And it was even less dark than it is today in those early days.

An equally plausible theory is that the 'Black' stands not for the colour of the kilt, but for the black Hanoverian hearts of the wearers of the kilt. Black as the pit, black as the forest of Rannoch, blacklegs, they must have seemed to the rebellious Jacobite clans. After all, non-Campbells in Scotland still talk cheerfully and automatically about 'black Campbells'. Or how about 'Black' for the Blackmail, which the Highland Watch was in business to suppress?

Anyway, the Black Watch did not become one of the Regiment's official names for more than a century. In 1725 they were called the Independent Highland Companies. Later they became the Highland Regiment of Foot. But right from the beginning they were known locally by the nick-name (possibly rude) of the 'Black Watch'.

Young Highlanders of quality and good family queued up to enlist in the Companies, because of the splendid status symbol of being allowed to carry arms. All other

Highlanders were forbidden to carry even a pistol by the Disarming Acts. Many of the Black Watch privates were related to their officers. An astonished English officer writes home, having seen the Black Watch: 'I cannot forbear to tell you that many of these private gentlemen soldiers have *gillies*, or servants, to attend them in quarters, and upon a march to carry their provisions, baggage, and firelocks'. Apparently privates used to ride up to the parade ground, followed by servants carrying their arms and their kit.

General David Stewart of Garth, the first of the long literary line of the Regiment's scholars and historians, writes of his great-uncle, who was one of these original gentleman rankers: 'This gentleman, a man of family and education, was five feet eleven inches in height, remarkable for his personal strength and activity, and one of the best swordsmen of his time', in an age when swordsmanship was the indispensable accomplishment of a gentleman. Yet for all this, 'he was only the centre man of the centre rank of his Company'. The Black Watch was an élite corps, fully trained in arms before it was recruited.

The Independent Companies all had their pipers, dressed in the very bright red tartan known as Stewart or Royal. This was because 'the Highland men would hardly be brought to march without it'—the bagpipes. General Wade ordered them to enlist a drummer as well. He felt, oddly, that the drum was a more martial instrument. In one of the Companies there was a fearful argument between the piper and the drummer about who should march in the place of honour as right marker. It ended with the piper crying: 'Ods wuds, Sir, and shall a little rascal that beats upon a sheepskin tak the right hand of me that am a musician?'

The six Companies were posted in detachments all over the Highland counties.

In 1739 war with Spain loomed because of Captain Jenkins's ear, and other weightier matters. So King

George II ordered that the Independent Highland Companies be incorporated into a Regiment of Foot, 'the men to be natives of that country, and none other to be taken'. The first Colonel, according to the documents, was to be 'Our Right Trusty and Right Well-Beloved Cousin, John, Earl of Craufurd and Lindsay'. The Earl of Crawford was in fact a Lowlander, the only one in his Regiment. Perhaps this was to avoid jealousy among the touchy Highlanders if a man from some other clan, infinitely inferior to their own, had been put in command of them. There is a bogus theory that the Black Watch tartan was invented for the new Colonel, because, being a Lowlander, he didn't have one of his own.

The first proud parade of The Highland Regiment, 10 companies, 850 strong, the fore-runner of the many famous Regiments to be raised in later years in the Highlands, was held in a field by the Tay near Aberfeldy, just by one of General Wade's stalwart bridges. A stirring statue of an ancient private soldier of the Highlanders stands in this field today. His name was Farquar Shaw, the son of a Strathspey laird. And he was 'a perfect swordsman and a deadly shot alike with the musket and pistol, and was known to twist a horse-shoe, and drive his dirk in a pine log'.

The private of the new Regiment was a formidable figure. He wore light buckled pumps or brogues, in which he could run like a mountain hare over the heather. His red and white chequered stockings were fastened with a broad red garter at the knee. A tartan 'belted plaid' 12 yards long was draped around his body like Cicero's toga, acting as a combined great-coat, tent, blanket, cloak, groundsheet, and umbrella. Plaid is Gaelic for blanket.

To put it on, you laid the ox-leather belt flat on the ground. Then you placed your plaid across the belt, pleating it neatly, and leaving a bit at each end unpleated. You then laid yourself carefully down on top of the pile, and fastened the belt around your middle by its silver buckle. The lower part of the plaid below the belt became the kilt when you stood up, the unpleated part being the apron of the kilt. The upper part sagged down over the belt, and was fastened up to the left shoulder with a pin. New recruits to the Regiment these days moan about being confined to barracks until they learn to wear the kilt properly. They don't realize how simple an operation it is now, compared with the good old days.

The sporran was made of badger, doe, otter, seal, or deer skin, with the hair outside. The original Highland soldier also wore a scarlet waistcoat, a short scarlet jacket with buff facings, and various fancy trimmings of white lace. On his head he had a flat blue pancake bonnet, with a border of red.

He carried a musket (officers had 'fuzils'), a broadsword with a basket handle, and a bayonet. Highland pistols, a target, and a dirk were optional extras. Most of them carried dirks. Sergeants had their grim 7-foot long Lochaber axes. And to answer the everlasting, tedious English question about what goes on underneath the kilt— In the early days of the Regiment some Highlanders were wrecked, and landed in France. A horrified local letter-writer reports on the kilt: 'Il y est très véridique qu'ils sont sans culotte dessous'. This is still the position.

Inevitably King George was keen to inspect the uniform of his new Regiment. Two privates 'remarkable for their figure and good looks' went down to London, and performed manual and platoon exercises in front of His Majesty, the Duke of Cumberland, and General Wade, in the great gallery of St. James's Palace. They were the first kilted troops ever seen in the capital, and inspired great gratification in the King's sartorially sensitive soul. At the end of the performance they were each tipped a guinea. Which caused huff and umbrage. As they left, the haughty Highlanders tossed their guineas to the porter at the

Palace gates. 'They believed, honest gentlemen, that the King had mistaken their condition in their own country'.

A famous Black Watch character of this period is Donald Macleod of Skye. He gave up the rank and pay of a sergeant in the Royal Scots, to join the new Highland Regiment as a private. And for no less than 75 years Donald served as a regular soldier in all of Britain's many wars around the world. He chased Highland robbers, fought duels, loved, married, and begot children, and when 103 years old was settled in London telling stories of the brave days, and grumbling about the meanness of the Government. At this stage his eldest son was 83, and his youngest 9.

For the next three years the Regiment carried on as before, keeping close watch on the Jacobite hills. Then in 1743 they were ordered south. They mustered at Perth for the long march to London. The Highlanders took a distinctly dim view of this. Many of them most powerfully and potently believed that they had been enlisted for service in the Highlands only, limited 'to the mountains', not for Sassenach expeditions. That was how it used to be in the days of the Independent Companies. They were partially pacified by being told that they were just going south to be reviewed by King George in corpulent person. In fact they were bound for Flanders, where the British army was locked in a ferocious, muddled war about who should succeed to the throne of Austria.

Morale was not improved when the King left for the Continent without inspecting them on the very day that the Regiment reached London. The English however were enthusiastic about the Black Watch. A newspaper of the day says: 'They are certainly the finest Regiment in the service, being tall, well-made men, and very stout'. Stout, one supposes, means hearty rather than obese.

Mischievous anti-Hanoverian visitors to the Highlanders' camps in the rural villages of Highgate and

Finchley spread subversive rumours. The Regiment was to be sent to the West Indies, they whispered; that feverish and fiery posting which was notorious as a grave of British soldiers. The Highlanders brooded dourly. They complained that 'after being used as rods to scourge their own countrymen, they were to be thrown into the fire'.

On the King's birthday, May 14, General Wade reviewed the Highlanders on Finchley Common. A paper of the day reported: 'The Highlanders made a very handsome appearance, and went through their exercise and firing with the utmost exactness. The novelty of the sight drew together the greatest concourse of people ever seen on such an occasion'.

After the review nearly 200 disgruntled Highlanders decided to desert, and force their way back to Scotland. At midnight they slid stealthily out of camp, taking their arms, and fourteen rounds of ball-cartridge each. They set off north. Panic and perturbation rippled out across the country at the news. What desperate deeds would these 'savage mountaineers' commit on the defenceless Home Counties? The ignorant English considered the Highlander to be 'a fierce and savage depredator, speaking a barbarous language, and inhabiting a barren and gloomy region, which fear and prudence alike forbade all strangers to enter'.

Despatches were rushed off in a cloud of dust to all officers commanding in northern districts ordering them to intercept the fugitives. A reward of 40s. was offered for each captured deserter. The retreat was led by a Corporal Samuel Macpherson, with considerable skill and strategy. The Highlanders marched mostly by night. By day they lay low, holed up in woods and strong defensive positions. They kept to the open country between the two great northern roads. And continually, foxily, they zig-zagged their line of march.

Conflicting reports and contradictory sightings poured

The mutineers are marched to the Tower after their capture.

in to the puzzled authorities. Four days later the Highlanders were camped during daylight in a very strong
position in Lady Wood, a hill four miles from Oundle.
A surreptitious game-keeper spotted them. And just before
noon squadrons of cavalry clattered as remorseless as fate
up to the foot of the hill. There was a long parley about a
free pardon. It lasted all day. The deserters were dug in too
tight to be dislodged by the troopers, and were determined
to die to the last man if they did not get a pardon. At last
during the darkness and doubt of night, the Highlanders
blew the powder out of their pans, and laid down their
arms.

The deserters had behaved with such discipline during
their retreat that public opinion now wheeled round full
circle, from terror to hero-worship. The escape was compared to the retreat of the Ten Thousand. Corporal
Macpherson was called a second Xenophon.

However, the stern military code of the day took a less enthusiastic view. 139 of them were tried for mutiny by general court-martial, found guilty, and condemned to be shot. The evidence at the trial, which had to be interpreted from Gaelic, shows that the poor fellows had only the foggiest idea what their 'mutiny' was all about. Indeed 79 of them couldn't speak a word of English. They all felt that the Government had cheated them villainously by bringing them out of the Highlands.

Private George Grant gave evidence: 'I am neither a Whig nor Papist, but I will serve the King for all that. I am not afraid; I never saw the man I was afraid of. I will not be cheated, nor do anything by trick. I will not be

Private Farquar Shaw, shot in the Tower for mutiny.

transported to the plantations, like a thief and a rogue'. Private John Stewart: 'I did not desert. I only wanted to go back to my own country because they abused me, and said I was to be transported. I had no leader or commander; we had not one man over the rest. We were all determined not to be tricked. We will all fight the French and Spaniards, but will not go like rogues to the plantations. I am not a Presbyterian. No, nor a Catholic.'

Corporal Samuel Macpherson, his brother Malcolm, and Private Farquar Shaw (the one who could straighten horse-shoes with his bare hands) were shot on Tower Hill. A newspaper of the day reports: 'The rest of the Highlanders were drawn out to see the execution, and joined in

Piper MacDonald, deported to Georgia for his part in the great mutiny, 1743.

prayer with great earnestness. The unfortunate men behaved with perfect resolution and propriety. Their bodies were put into three coffins by three of their clansmen and namesakes, and buried in one grave near the place of execution'.

The rest of the deserters were drafted to other Regiments serving in plague-spots a thousand miles from their purple hills. Up in the Highlands the men who had been punished were generally regarded as martyrs to the treachery of the Government. This indignation may well have helped the cause of Bonnie Prince Charlie two years later. Certainly, if the Black Watch had been stationed in Aberfeldy instead of in Flanders, the adventures of 1745 might have had a quicker ending.

A mutiny is not normally the most conventional or rosy beginning to the history of a Regiment. But then this was hardly a normal mutiny. The Colonel of the Highlanders four years later kept portraits of the three ring-leaders hanging in his dining-room. Either because he thought they had been 'ignorantly misled rather than wilfully culpable'. Or else to preserve pictures of men 'who were remarkable for their size and handsome figure'.

Whatever his motive, the Colonel does not seem to have felt that the great 'mutiny' was so disgraceful that it must be buried in black oblivion, never to be spoken of again. In any case, whatever blot was made on the Regiment's record by this its first and only mutiny, was very soon wiped away by blood, battle, and bravery beyond the call of loyalty.

Chapter 2

THE REMAINDER OF THE Regiment, brought up to a strength of 900, arrived in Flanders in June 1743 to join the allied army under King George II in the War of the Austrian Succession. They were the first kilted unit seen on the Continent. And in the next two years of manœuvring the Black Watch collected itself some testimonials which can only be described as glowing. An English Colonel wrote that the Regiment 'was regarded as a trustworthy guard of property. Seldom were any of the men of it seen drunk, and they as seldom swore'. Maybe he did not understand Gaelic. And the Elector Palatine thanked King George in a letter for the behaviour of the Black Watch while in his tiny kingdom, 'for whose sake I shall always pay a regard to a Scotsman in future'.

In 1745 the thundering cannons roared for the Black Watch's bloody baptism of fire at Fontenoy. Marshal Saxe with a French army of 80,000 was besieging Tournay. Against him moved that obese Martial Boy, the Duke of Cumberland, then aged 25, with 50,000 men. In the preliminary skirmishing the Highlanders cleared a village with sword and dirk. And one Jock hung his bonnet on a stick to divert the attention of a French sharp-shooter, stalked him from behind, and shot him. This tactic seems to have been revolutionary, and excited comment from the old soldiers.

On the morning of the battle the troops started forming up long before crack of dawn. The French were deeply dug in on the four-mile-long crest of a hill. In the wood to their left front they had built a redoubt or prefabricated fortress, whose guns enfiladed the hill up which the British must advance.

The Brigade of which the Black Watch was part was ordered to silence this redoubt before the general advance. Because of some muddle in the O-group, for which the Brigadier was afterwards court-martialled, they omitted to do this. The white-hot Duke of Cumberland decided to carry on regardless. And the British army in three lines, with the Black Watch on the extreme right, set off up a thousand yards of hill, into shot and steel and scorching flame from three sides. Pipes droned. They marched into the murderous cross-fire, with arms shouldered, at the slow, nonchalant pace which the British had made famous through Europe. They marched up into the cannon's mouth, until they were eyeball to eyeball, 30 yards from the French trenches.

The Black Watch had received permission to fight in their own Highland way. So, as soon as the volleying muskets of the French played along the line, they hurled themselves to the ground—all except their Lieutenant-Colonel, who was so fat that if he once lay down, he could not get to his feet again without help. Then, once the volley was over, they leaped to their feet and fired back. The other British Regiments, fighting in the traditional English stiff-upper-lip way, received the French fire standing in line like skittles—one Guardsman even shouted, just before the French fired: 'For what we are about to receive may the Lord make us truly thankful.'

A Black Watch Sergeant called James Campbell killed nine French with his broadsword, and had his arm removed by a cannon-ball while having a swipe to get his score into double figures. The Duke of Cumberland was so impressed that he promised him a reward after the battle 'of a value equal to the arm'.

'But bring a Scotsman frae his hill—
Clap in his cheek a Highland gill—
Say such is Royal George's will,
    An' there's the foe—
He has one thocht but how to kill
    Twa at a blow.'

The Black Watch Chaplain was seen at the head of the column with a drawn sword. The Colonel ordered him to the rear with the surgeons, unless he wanted to have his commission cancelled. The Chaplain, who had as much

Sergeant James Campbell of the Highland Regiment who killed nine Frenchmen with his broadsword at Fontenoy in 1745, and lost his arm while making a stroke for the tenth.

influence as the Colonel in a Regiment of devout High-landers, replied: 'Damn my commission'.

After a day of terrible pounding, after the French House-hold Cavalry had been shivered to fragments on what a Frenchman described as the 'flaming fortresses' of the British infantry columns, Saxe brought up fresh troops, and the British had to retire back down the blood-stained hill. The Black Watch were among those chosen to cover the retreat, because they were the least disordered of the Regiments engaged. They had only 135 casualties and missing, perhaps because of their sensible habit of lying down when shot at.

When it was over, the Brigadier in charge of the with-drawal 'pulled off his hat, and returning them thanks, said that they had acquired as much honour in covering so great a retreat, as if they had gained the battle'. A French pamphlet about Fontenoy says: ' . . . the Highland furies rushed in upon us with more violence than ever did a sea driven by a tempest'. According to a contemporary British pamphlet: 'Their courage was the theme of admiration through all Britain'.

Later, the bard Dugald Dhu summed the whole affair up very adequately, though with a slight touch of Toad of Toad Hall braggadocio:

> 'Hail, gallant regiment, Freiceadan Dubh;
> Whenever Albion needs thine aid,
> 'Aye ready' for whatever foe
> Shall dare to meet the 'Black Brigade'.
> Witness disastrous Fontenoy,
> When all seemed lost, who brought us through?
> Who saved defeat, secured retreat?
> And bore the brunt? The "Forty-Two".'

in fact at Fontenoy the Regiment was numbered the 43rd.

There is some interesting evidence from these days about the peculiarly democratic relationship between officers and

men in a Regiment in which everyone was related to everyone else. Once there was a vacancy because the Colonel
had been promoted. The men came forward with a large
sum of money subscribed among themselves to purchase
the Lieutenant-Colonelcy for their own Major Grant,
rather than see the job go to someone outside the Regiment. In the event the money was not needed, because the
promotion went inside the Black Watch, without purchase.
There were also occasions in these early years when the
men felt that an officer had let them down by inefficiency
or misconduct in the field, although he had not been
publicly censured by his superiors. But the men made
formal representations that they could not and would not
remain any longer under his command.

In the autumn of 1745 the Black Watch was hurriedly
brought home to help cope with Prince Charles Edward
and his supporters. Mercifully the Regiment was not sent
north to fight against its own kith and kin. Instead it was
stationed in Kent to defend the coast against a suspected
invasion. For the next three years the Black Watch was
engaged in a series of feeble and fruitless descents upon
France and Flanders. In 1749 the Highland Regiment
received by Royal Warrant the Regimental Number
'42nd'; a number destined to crop up persistently in the
battles fought by Britain around the world. From 1749
to 1756 the Regiment was stationed in Ireland, keeping
'watch' on the natives, with whom the Highlanders got on
famously. The Regimental records show regular daily
prayers, and very few courts-martial. The privates apparently with clannish pride enforced their own discipline
among themselves. And the Regiment was 'a school of
virtue as well as a fighting force'.

In 1756 the Black Watch began its long and close con-
nection with North America, which has lasted down the
centuries. The Regiment sailed to New York to help the
British colonists in their war against the French, who were

operating from their base in Canada. The Red Indians received them with open arms, as blood brothers. For some obscure reason, they believed that the Highlanders were distant long-lost relatives of their own.

In 1758 a great British expedition set off up the Hudson and the lakes leading to Montreal from the south. The Marquis de Montcalm with a much smaller French force blocked their road at Fort Ticonderoga, at the junction of two lakes. Here the French had built a massive breastwork of trees, defended with an impenetrable entanglement of branches and sharpened stakes. The English General, James Abercromby, had a number of useful options. He could have made a flanking attack on the blind side of the fort. He could have brought up his artillery, and blasted it to sawdust. Or he could have just by-passed it, and marched on to Montreal, cutting Montcalm's lines of communication.

The Highlanders attack the French breastwork at Ticonderoga, 1758.

Instead, after a cursory reconnaissance, he ordered a frontal assault with bayonet and broadsword. The High-landers were in reserve. In the blazing noon the troops could hardly force their way through the maze of tangled trees. Invisible muskets poured shot into them from behind the breastwork. After an hour of agony they reported back to the General, who was sitting in a saw-mill near his artillery two miles away, that the fort was impregnable. His only reply was 'Attack again'.

The Black Watch, 'with a fury that would yield neither to discipline nor to death', rushed forward from their position in reserve without waiting for orders. They hacked a way with their broadswords up to the 10-foot high breastwork. A handful of Highlanders managed to climb the wooden wall by standing on each others shoulders. They were instantly bayoneted.

One of the Highlanders there on that long day later described the fearsome French barricade:

'Thousands of trees, the tops lopped off and the trunks piled one upon another. It was so high that nothing could be seen over it but the crowns of the soldiers hats. Sods and bags of sand were piled along the top, with narrow spaces to fire through. Along the front of the breastworks the ground was covered with heavy boughs, overlapping and interlaced, with sharpened points bristling into the face of an assailant like quills of a porcupine'.

The desperate, lunatic struggle went on for four hours, 'until the inner abatis was hung with wisps of scarlet, like poppies that grow through a hedge of thorn'. Even then the order to retreat had to be given three times before the Highlanders would leave their fallen comrades. The Black Watch again covered the retreat. There is some truth as well as swagger in the old Regimental boast—'Freiceadan Dubh nan cath; toiseach tighinn is deireadh falbh'—'The Black Watch of the Battles; first to come (in the attack) and last to go (in the retreat)'.

The 42nd lost twice as many as any other Regiment engaged, 314 killed and 333 wounded. Only at Loos in 1915, where the 9th Battalion lost 701 in a day, has the Black Watch ever had heavier casualties. An officer of the Regiment wrote afterwards: 'The affair at Fontenoy was nothing to it—I saw both. So much determined bravery can scarcely be paralleled. Even those who lay mortally wounded cried aloud to their companions not to mind or waste a thought upon them, but to follow their officers, and remember the honour of their country. Nay, their ardour was such that it was difficult to bring them off. When shall we have so fine a Regiment again?'

The Black Watch has its own scalp-tingling ghost story about Ticonderoga. Years before, Duncan Campbell of Inverawe gave refuge to a Stewart who was being hunted through his glen—bad territory for Stewarts. He swore on his dirk not to give him up, and he kept his oath, even when he was told that this particular Stewart had just murdered his cousin, Donald Campbell.

That night the ghost of cousin Donald appeared at the foot of his bed, and begged him to avenge his foul murder. Duncan refused, because of his oath. The ghost said: 'Very well, Inverawe. We shall meet again at Ticonderoga'.

> 'He heard the outlandish name;
> It sang in his sleeping ears,
> It hummed in his waking head;
> The name—Ticonderoga,
> The utterance of the dead.'

Nobody in Scotland had ever heard of the strange name. Duncan joined the Black Watch. And one day he arrived with the Regiment before Montcalm's fort. Somebody mentioned casually that the Mohawk Indians had a strange name for the place, 'Ticonderoga'. Duncan said: 'That means I shall die tomorrow'. And sure enough, the next

Captain John Campbell of Melford wounded at Ticonderoga, painted in the uniform of 1762.

day, in the thickest of the fighting, Duncan was mortally wounded by a musket ball.

Just before the battle the King gave the Regiment the title of Royal. It was now officially called The 42nd (Royal Highland) Regiment, and its facings were therefore changed from buff to royal blue.

In 1758 a 2nd Battalion of the Royal Highland Regiment was raised. It sailed straight to the fever and sweat of the West Indies, and fought at Martinique and Guadeloupe, among the trailing mangrove roots. Bomb-ketches launched their flaming missiles into the black velvet tropical darkness; and the 2nd Battalion had to fight a

French lady at the head of a column of her armed slaves. In 1759 they joined up with the skeleton of the 1st Battalion on Lake Ontario, and both Battalions helped to storm Ticonderoga. The wooden fortress which had cost so much blood the year before fell in only half an hour. The fort at Ticonderoga has been restored, and made into a museum with many Black Watch associations.

In 1760, after a hazardous navigation of the rapids of the St. Lawrence, both Battalions shared in the capture of Montreal. This brought the whole of Canada into British hands. Next year both Battalions were posted back to the West Indies. An order says that the Royal Highlanders were particularly suitable for this service, because 'their sobriety and abstemious habits', and their toughness made them able to bear the rough climate and country better than other Regiments. They fought side by side to add Martinique and the Windward Islands to Britain's compulsive collection of tropical islands. In 1762 they both joined in the attack on 'The Havannah' in Cuba, the Spanish storehouse for the precious metals of Peru and Mexico which has now become the capital of the island. After a 40-day siege and great hardships of humid heat and tropical disease, they finally stormed the formidable harbour fortress of Havana called the 'Moro', and brought home the wealth of the Indies. The Jocks who had done the digging each received £4 prize money from this great treasure-house of Spain. The General collected £122,000.

After Cuba the 2nd Battalion was amalgamated into the 1st, and the Royal Highlanders went back to five years of patrolling on the wild, not-so-far-west frontier of North America. They fought a classic Red Indian battle at Bushy Run in 1763. Here they were ambushed and surrounded for days by 'savages skipping nimbly from tree to tree'. The Highlanders formed a circle round their wounded and pack horses. The Indians charged again and again at dawn

Ambushed by Red Indians at Bushy Run, 1763.

and dusk with wild Geronimo whoops. Dim drums
throbbed through the night. Finally the Highlanders made
a feint as if they were going to try to break out. The
Indians rushed in for the kill, and were themselves ambushed and wiped out. A cynical historian writes: 'Only
the dread of being roasted alive kept the exhausted troops
at their work'.

A remarkable character in these back-woods campaigns
was Lieutenant-Colonel John Reid of the Black Watch.
'The men of the 42nd were much attached to him for his
poetry, his music, and his bravery as a soldier'. He was one
of the most accomplished flute players of the age, and
composed the pipe tune 'The Highland March', which was
later given the words 'In the garb of Old Gaul'. He became
a General, and when he died left £50,000 to establish the
Chair of Music at Edinburgh University.

In 1767 the Regiment sailed to Ireland. Uniforms by
now were very dingy. Old brick-dust red jackets were
patched into waistcoats. And the men paid for their own

hose, rather than wear the shoddy kit provided by the Government. The men also supplied out of their own pockets ostrich feathers for their bonnets instead of the shabby piece of black bear-skin issued by the Government. The Colonel gave them white goat-skin sporrans instead of their original badger-skin ones. In 1768 the Regiment was given its present motto, 'Nemo me impune lacessit', and something like its present badge with St. Andrew and his cross.

At last, in 1775, after more than 30 years' absence, the Highlanders came home to Scotland. As they approached the shore, many of the old soldiers leaped out of the boats 'with tears of joy, kissed their native earth with enthusiasm, and grasped it in handfuls'. At this point there were 931 Highlanders in the Regiment, 74 Lowlanders, 2 Irishmen, 1 Welshman—and 5 Englishmen in the band. The official height standard was 5 foot 7 inches. But a few men under 5 foot 5 inches were hidden away in the centre rank. 'They were frequently able to undergo greater fatigues than the biggest men in the corps'. In spite of strenuous objections all round, three English officers received commissions in the Black Watch this year.

In 1776 came the American War of Independence, and the Regiment was sent back across the Atlantic to fight against its recent allies, the wild colonial boys under George Washington. The Black Watch gets into hot water with distressing regularity when it is at sea. This time one of the transports was captured by an American privateer. The Highlanders recaptured the ship from the American prize-crew, and steered it straight into a port— which turned out to have just been occupied by the American rebels. The rest of the 42nd eventually reached New York. About this time broadswords and pistols were withdrawn from the Highlanders; one reason given was that the swords kept on getting entangled in thick woods. There were passionate protests from the traditionalists.

'Nothing like a good broadsword charge to break up an enemy who has stood up to musketry all day', and so on.

The Black Watch fought in the successful battle of Brooklyn, close to where sky-scrapers now bristle. But the British Generals and British tactics were too hidebound. The success was not followed up. And Washington slipped clean away. At Bloomingdale and White Plains later in the year it was the same story. The British troops won an initial success. The Highlanders dragged a very fat Major of their's called Murray up cliff and down precipice like a sack of potatoes, while he cried to them on no account to leave him behind. But the more versatile American troops dodged and buzzed like wasps around the lumbering British bulldog army, with its formal ideas of war and equipment.

In 1777 the Americans surprised the Black Watch in camp at Pisquatua. A Sergeant Macgregor was severely wounded. He happened to be wearing a new jacket with silver lace, and big silver buckles on his shoes. One of the Americans liked the look of all this silver. So rather than strip the Highlander on the spot, he picked him up on his back, and staggered off to the woods and a bit of privacy. Unfortunately for him, the Sergeant recovered. He pulled out his dirk, and threatened to let some air into the American's back, if he did not turn round and carry him straight back into the 42nd's camp. The unhappy American headed back to the camp, where he bumped into the Colonel of the Black Watch. The Colonel thanked him for looking after his Sergeant so well, and let him go free.

Later in the year the Black Watch were engaged in the for once pitched, and for once comparatively victorious battle of Brandywine. And here, quite probably, they first wore their famous and mysterious red hackle. For years the Highlanders had been decorating their bonnets with assorted feathers, perhaps in imitation of their Red Indian 'brothers'. There is a misty story of this period of the

Americans, after some bitter engagement, saying they would take no prisoners next time. And before Brandywine the Black Watch and two other British Regiments who had been involved sent back word to the effect 'Very well, just so that you'll know us, we'll be wearing red feathers in our bonnets'.

In 1779 a dreadful draft of 150 men, 'for the most part the sweepings of London and Dublin', was sent out to the Regiment. 'They were of the most depraved character, and of habits so dissolute that one half of them were unfit for service'. And they seem to have diluted the stern old Highland morale of the Regiment for a year or two. The war limped to an ignominious end in 1782, and the United States became independent. The histories record that during the five years of the war the Highlanders were so temperate that they only drew their rum ration every fourth day. All the other Regiments drew it thirstily every day. The Highlanders were not so abstemious about nicotine however. The reason that a wooden figure of a Highlander in Black Watch uniform used to stand in all good tobacconist shops, is that the tobacconists of London were so amazed and delighted at the Regiment's capacity for snuff.

The 2nd Battalion had been raised again in 1779, when the three corners of the world in arms were coming together against Britain. An advertisement in a paper of that year offers 5 guineas for recruits. 'You who, uncorrupted by the universal depravity of your southern countrymen, have withstood, unmoveable as a rock, all the assaults of Surrounding Luxury and Dissipation. You who, while others, effeminated by voluptuous refinements, and irrecoverably lost to honour, lolling in the arms of Pleasure, can see the danger of their country with a criminal indifference . . .' etc. This time the 2nd Battalion, instead of joining up with the 1st, went off to India to make some history of its own.

The 1st Battalion sailed to Nova Scotia in 1783, and

then on to Cape Breton in Canada three years later. In 1789 the Highlanders returned to Portsmouth, and marched up to Northumberland. This took them a month. The next year they were stationed in Glasgow, where the citizens were so hospitable with their drams 'that the discipline of the Regiment became somewhat relaxed'. They were removed from the temptations of 'ardent spirits' to Edinburgh Castle in the autumn. Then the Black Watch had three years in the Highlands, being used in the ugly work of Highland clearances, ejecting crofters from their cottages to make room for the big landlords.

In 1794 Britain was at war with the Revolutionary Government of France. After various alarums and excursions and abortive expeditions across the Channel and to Guernsey, the Black Watch landed in Flanders. It was a shivering, frozen winter, and the troops had no greatcoats. At the battle of Geldermalsen in 1795 there is a mythical legend that the Black Watch won its red hackle. The myth is that some Light Dragoons, wearing a red hackle, abandoned a couple of guns to the French in front of the Highlanders. The General called out: 'Forty-Second, for God's sake and for the honour of your country, retake those guns'. The Black Watch recovered the guns with severe losses, and were rewarded with the red hackle of the Light Dragoons. The Dragoons were given a white hackle in exchange. To come down to earth, the Black Watch in fact, only lost one man in this battle, and the vivid story was built on a foundation of painted smoke.

What is true is that when the Black Watch returned home from the campaign, the first official issue of the 'Red Vulture Feathers' was made to the Regiment on parade at Royston in Hertfordshire. The red hackle probably came from those long years in North America. And in an Army Order of 1822 the Adjutant-General confirmed that the Red Vulture Feather 'is intended to be worn exclusively by the Forty-Second Regiment'.

Later in 1795 the Black Watch joined the biggest expeditionary force ever to sail from Britain up to that date, against the French West Indies. Britain was using the French war as an excuse to add to its collection of tropical islands. The Highlanders were issued with 'Russia duck pantaloons and round hats' instead of their kilts and bonnets. It was felt that this mysterious uniform would be a better protection against the vertical sun, the yellow fever, and particularly the mosquitoes. On the subject of this sartorial change 'there was no little controversy'.

As usual when the Black Watch were on board, a storm scattered the fleet of 300 ships. Five companies and the Headquarters ended up in Gibraltar. Several thousand miles away from H.Q. the other five companies took part in the capture of St. Lucia and St. Vincent, where there was some stiff fighting. The Caribs ran up trees and shot down from the thick foliage. One of these snipers shot down by a Jock turned out to be a woman 'in tight-fitting rose-coloured silk trousers'.

In 1798 the five companies rejoined their comrades in Gibraltar, 'where the character of the troops was sensibly deteriorated under the temptation of drink'. The Black Watch ended the century, most of which they had spent skirmishing and bushwhacking on the fringes of civilization, by assisting in the capture of Minorca in 1798; by sailing backwards and forwards in the Mediterranean as sea-sick marines; to Malta, and back to Gibraltar again. In 1800 they made an attack on Cadiz, and retreated rapidly when they discovered that plague was raging in the town.

Chapter 3

THIS INDECISIVE marine life lasted for some months. A troop-ship in those days was a half-armed, unseaworthy two-decker, full of sea-sickness, discontent, and doubt about its destination. Then with a bang the Black Watch bumped into the new century and the Napoleonic wars. They landed at Aboukir Bay off Alexandria in March, 1801, with the British expeditionary force under General Sir Ralph Abercromby.

It was a famous and fortunate sea-borne invasion. As soon as the fleet dropped anchor in the bay, yet another wild gale sprang up and prevented a landing for a week. The triumphant French army in Egypt, waiting on the shore, out-numbered the British by two to one. The little Corsican Corporal was not among those present, having had to hurry back to France on business. But his army was much stronger than the British in guns and cavalry. It knew the country. It was hardened to the sand and the sun. And it could see exactly where the invaders were going to land. The British were unable even to reconnoitre which was the best beach for a landing because of the gale.

Nevertheless, as soon as the gale blew itself out, at two in the morning the British tumbled into their boats, 60 soldiers to a boat, and pulled in perfect formation for the shore. The Black Watch were in the middle of the first wave of 5,000, sitting packed together like pilchards, in light marching order, each man with his musket between his knees.

The sea spluttered to spindrift with round shot and grape from the shore batteries. The Highlanders hit the beach at the foot of some steep sandy cliffs with French guns and a Battalion of infantry dug in along the top. The Regiment formed up in line. Muskets crackled. The order 'Fix Bayonets' was given. Then 'Prime and Load'. At once a voice from the ranks cried: 'No prime and load, but charge baignets, immediately'. The voice belonged to Private Donald Black, an old smuggler from Skye. The Black Watch took off as one man, charged up the cliffs, and cleared the French position with cold steel. The landing at Aboukir has been described as a victory 'almost without parallel in the annals of war'. The 42nd lost 190 killed and wounded.

A fortnight later, after skirmishing, and discovering that Highland bonnets and shoes are not the most sensible gear for the desert, came the inevitable battle, at Alexandria. The Black Watch were on the right of the British line, beside a ruined palace of the Ptolemies by the sea, from whose summit 40 centuries looked down on the battle. At three in the morning a volley of musketry from the French dromedary corps far away on the left crackled the beginning of the battle. But it was only a feint. The full fury of the French attack fell on the British right wing, towards the ancient ruins where the Highlanders were posted.

It was a night as black as coal. Drifting smoke stung the eyes. A column of crack French Grenadiers, known as 'The Invincibles', infiltrated silently down a sandy gully between the Black Watch and their next door neighbours, a Regiment of Foot-Guards. The trundle of the French six-pounder was muffled in the sand. A Black Watch Private saw these shadowy ghosts creeping past, and called to his Captain. The Captain ran forward, and heard the ghosts dressing their line in French. The Black Watch faced to the right in a hurry, and charged. With bayonet and butt-end and desperate mêlée the Invincibles were driven into the ancient ruins. A Black Watch Private who was there wrote afterwards that the French 'chocked themselves like cattle forced in at a gate'. The French officer carrying their standard fell, shouting over and over: 'Vive la République'. Most of his gallant men were chopped down. And their colour was captured by a Major of the Black Watch.

A great force of enemy infantry now came up against the Royal Highlanders, who were in an unregimental jumble, hurrying to get out of the ruins, and lengthen their line. The Commander-in-Chief, General Sir Ralph Abercromby, called out 'My brave Highlanders, remember your country. Remember your forefathers'. The French were driven back, and the Highlanders started to chase them.

It was now nearly daylight. And out of the distance, out of the dawn suddenly appeared three squadrons of French cavalry drawn up to charge. The Highlanders were hastily ordered to reform in a new position. But the orders were not heard by every company in the hubbub of battle. So the rash and daring French horsemen came thundering in 'with the impetuosity of a torrent' on a Regiment whose line was already broken and disorganized. But the 42nd rallied, and stood firm in their isolated hedgehog groups, bristling with bayonets. Apparently they were expert at bringing down the horse before the rider came within sword-length, and then polishing off the rider with the bayonet. More cavalry charges were repulsed. The British cavalry, who should have been in support of the Black Watch, were held up by the many pits which the soldiers had dug in the sand for their 'camp kettles'.

It was only eight in the morning, but the night's work had been so hot that the Black Watch had run out of ammunition. French cannon-shot bounced over the billiard-table desert, and carried off a file of men with every ricochet. But at last the tide of battle turned, and the

French began to retreat into defeat. General Abercromby was nearly captured by two French cavalrymen early on in the battle. He was seen 'cutting behind and before just like a youth of twenty'. A Black Watch Corporal came to his rescue in the nick of time.

After the battle the General was found to be sorely wounded. A musket-ball was lodged deep in his hip. He was carried off on a litter, with a blanket belonging to a Black Watch Private wrapped up as a pillow under his head. He died a week later. There was no other means of embalming him, so his body was put into a hogshead of rum to be carried home to Britain. The barrel leaked. And the General had to be buried in Malta, in the fort at the mouth of Valetta harbour.

In the battle the 42nd lost 54 killed and 261 wounded. Sir John Fortescue, the historian of the British army, writing about Alexandria, says that the Black Watch 'stands pre-eminent for a gallantry and steadfastness which would be difficult to match in the history of any army'. It

Battle of Alexandria, 1801. In the centre a Black Watch Corporal comes to the rescue of the Commander-in-Chief, General Abercromby. On the right, the ruined palace of the Ptolemies, where the rest of the Royal Highlanders are dealing with the Invincibles.

was in this campaign that the Regiment earned the battle honour of bearing the Sphinx with the word EGYPT as a badge on its colours. By mid-summer the French capitulated, and Egypt was won. The 42nd sailed home to Southampton, and were stationed at Winchester. In 1802 they were reviewed by the King and two of his sons at Ashford in Kent in front of an enormous crowd which had come from as far away as London.

For the next fifteen years the Regiment had a haughty family row with the Highland Society of Scotland. The Society wanted to present the Royal Highland Regiment with a superb silver vase, stiff with Sphinxes and symbolism. But there was unpleasantness about the colours of the Invincibles which the Black Watch had captured at Alexandria. The Sergeant looking after them had been knocked out later in the battle, and the French standard had been picked up and carried off by an enterprising German soldier, who now produced it with shrill cries of triumph. The Society asked for an explanation of the Black Watch's story. The Highlanders took offence at being asked. The umbrage lasted, and the vase remained at the makers until 1817.

In 1802 the Regiment marched north to Edinburgh. In 1803 a 2nd Battalion was again raised for the French wars. It was to have a short, sharp existence this time, being merged with the 1st Battalion in Spain in 1812, and disbanded in 1814. An eye-witness of this period describes a party of the 42nd recruiting in Paisley. The Sergeant, a proper Highlander, harangued his gaping audience: 'Noo, then, my praw lads, come awa', and list in this bauld, auld corps—often tried but neffer found wanting—and called the Twa-and-Forty Royal Hielandman's Fut and Plack Watches. Commanded by His Royal Grace, Prince Frederick, King o' the Hielands, and Emperor o' all the Europes in Scotland. And she'll gie ye the praw dress and the muckle money'.

He then pulled out a great bundle of money. A recruit came hurrying up, all eager for the treat. And the Sergeant counted out his bounty—'There, my praw lad—sax and twa's ten—awa wi' ye noo, you damned scoundrel'.

Both Battalions were together for a year in camp near Colchester. Then the 1st Battalion had its traditional rough sea passage to the great rock of Gibraltar. In 1808 British armies marched into Spain from three directions to meet at Salamanca on the road to Madrid. The Black Watch came up from the south in the pincer from Gibraltar. The idea was to join with the Spaniards to defeat Napoleon's huge army of occupation in Spain. It didn't work. Madrid fell, nerveless, to the French in a day. The slender and shambolic Spanish army was puffed out of existence. And at the appointed rendezvous where they had expected to meet their allies, the British force of 40,000 met with the dragoons and outlying skirmishers of a much bigger French army. The only hope was to try to evacuate as much of the British army as possible before it was annihilated. So on Christmas Eve Sir John Moore about-turned his columns westwards, and headed for his sea-base at Corunna, 250 miles away in the north-west corner of Spain, across wild mid-winter mountains. It was a desperate retreat. Black skies impended. Bitter tempests whipped the trudging troops. They were gnawed by hunger, shaken with the ague, bare-foot, and ragged. French dragoons hovered and harried around the fringes of the column. Discipline collapsed. Arms were thrown away. Soldiers shambled arm in arm, like drunks.

The Black Watch were in the rear-guard, and beat off the advance parties of the French in a number of successful, skin-of-the-teeth actions. The British army did not lose a gun or a flag on its long retreat. The kilt stood up to the savage weather better than other uniforms. And the Black Watch made themselves Highland shoes, or *cuarans*, out of the hides of dead horses. The retreat went on for 18 days,

'The consequences of not shifting the leg'—A Royal Highlander disposing of one of Napoleon's soldiers.

and 4,000 British died of exposure on it. When the survivors limped into Corunna, pipes playing past the General, the Regiments with fewest stragglers and casualties were the Guards, the Black Watch, and two other kilted Regiments.

At Corunna, in January 1809, the British army turned at bay to cover its embarkation. The hammer-blow of the French again fell on the Brigade of which the Royal Highlanders were part. Sir John Moore called out to them as the French attack started to come in: 'Highlanders, Remember Egypt'. Some accounts of the battle say that after fierce fighting three Companies of the 42nd ran out of ammunition, and began to fall back, thinking that a Regiment of Footguards was coming to relieve them. And the General is said to have shouted out again: 'My brave 42nd, join your comrades. Ammunition is coming, and you have your bayonets'. The Companies turned, and

47

closed again on the enemy with their bayonets. But there is considerable controversy about this episode, and it was emphatically denied after the battle by the Commanding Officer of the Black Watch. In any case, it is always slightly curious how these heroic quotations from Generals were ever heard in the din of battle.

Perhaps more authentic, a Private of the Black Watch wrote his worm's-eye-witness narrative of Corunna after the battle—'The Commanding Officer said "42nd Charge". In one moment every man was up with a cheer, and the sound of his musket, and every shot did execution. They were so close upon us that we gave them the bayonet the instant we fired. The confusion that now ensued baffles all my powers, even of memory and imagination—pell-mell, ding-dong—ilka man gat his birdie, and many of us skivered pairs, front and rear rank; to the right about they went, and we after them. I think I see the grizzly fellows now, running and jumping, as the Highlanders, laughing and swearing and foaming, stuck the pointed steel into

The Black Watch tumble the French down the hill at Corunna, 1809.

their loins. We followed them down the valley, and stopped not for General or Commanding Officer. But still on, in the rage and wrath of the Highlanders'.

The Commanding Officer of an English Regiment at Corunna wrote in his memoirs that when the battle started he had received no orders, and was in a quandary. He saw the Black Watch advancing, and shouted to one of his officers: 'Good God, Montgomery, are we not to advance?' Montgomery, a Scot, replied: 'I would not wait. You cannot be wrong to follow the 42nd'.

The battle was a brilliant success against heavy odds. But Sir John Moore was shattered by a cannon shot while watching the Black Watch advance. He was helped behind a wall by one of the Highlanders, and later carried off the field by four Royal Highlanders and two Guardsmen, 'shedding tears all the way'. He died that night. Moore, who shook the cobwebs of a century off out-of-date British military tactics, was a great admirer of the Black Watch. He said that their toughness made them able to stand fatigue under which other apparently stronger men would sink. He also said that their courage was sure, and not just a flash in the pan.

The evacuation went without a hitch now, and the Black Watch arrived in Kent, tattered, battered, and riddled with typhus, having suffered 212 casualties at Corunna.

In the summer the Regiment took part in the disastrous expedition to the island of Walcheren in Holland. 'The Earl of Chatham, with sword drawn, stood waiting for Sir Richard Strachan; Sir Richard, longing to be at 'em, was waiting for the Earl of Chatham'. In six weeks the dreaded Walcheren fever, malaria, reduced the strength of the Regiment from 758 to 204 fit men, with hardly a shot fired in anger. The Black Watch returned to Edinburgh to recuperate. For the first time recruiting was difficult. The ranks were filled up with Lowlanders and Irish. But the Regiment was still far under strength when it returned to

Portugal again in 1812 to join Wellington's army in his Peninsular campaign. The 2nd Battalion had already been there for three years, fighting on the long ridge of Busaco in 1810; in the lines of Torres Vedras; standing up in squares to charging cavalry at Fuentes d'Onoro in 1811; and storming the great citadel of Ciudad Rodrigo in 1812.

The 1st Battalion of the Royal Highlanders now arrived on the bloody Spanish scene, and was brought up to a strength of 1,160 by being merged with its 2nd Battalion. At Salamanca, in July 1812, the Black Watch took part in Wellington's favourite victory, that twisting cat-and-mouse battle which destroyed the French army. 'I never saw an army receive such a beating,' wrote the Iron Duke. The 42nd marched into Madrid with the rest of the allied army. 'Their pipers, and martial yet wild-looking garb attracted much attention, and a dense crowd of staring Spaniards squeezed along on the flanks of the Regiment, accompanying it through all the streets.'

Next the 42nd were splicing scaling-ladders together to storm the giddy heights of Burgos—an assault 'which no commander but Lord Wellington would have dared to order, and which no troops in the world but British troops would have dared to execute.' The castle's strength laughed the siege to scorn, and after 33 days the British left secretly by night, their artillery wheels muffled in straw. The unsuccessful assault had cost the Black Watch 297 casualties.

In 1813 the Highlanders fought at Vitoria, which drove the French back to the Pyrenees. There followed months of hard clambering through the great mountains onto French soil. The Black Watch stormed across those raging winter torrents, the Nivelle and the Nive, into the long French entrenchments, and embroidered their Colours with new names. The Regiment was by now very tattered, and losing the kilt by degrees. Men tied their ragged kilt into trousers, and there was no new plaid to make replacements.

In 1814, in February, they fought at Orthes, through mines and over pontoon bridges, tumbling the French cavalry down the rocky ground. In April they attacked the formidable fortifications of Toulouse. The battle hung on the razor-edge of whether the British could storm some heavy redoubts up a ridge on the French right.

The Brigade Commander rode up and said: 'The 42nd shall have the honour of leading the attack. The 42nd will advance.' The Highlanders charged up the hill over 300 yards of ploughed fields into the redoubts. 'We leaped over the trenches like a pack of hungry hounds in pursuit, frightening them more by our wild hurrahs than actually hurting them by ball or bayonet,' wrote a Lieutenant who led the way into the redoubts. The Colour was ripped to rags, and stained with the blood of the three officers who had been killed in rapid succession carrying it. A Sergeant carried it into the French lines. Of the 500 Royal Highlanders who went into action, scarcely 90 reached the fatal redoubts. Less than 60 were unwounded. The 42nd was one of the four Regiments particularly commended by Wellington after the battle. A French officer who watched the Black Watch advance into the torrent of fire up the slippery hill, said 'My God, how firm these sans culottes are'. A historian of Wellington wrote of the battle of Toulouse: 'It was a cluster of Scottish Regiments which, by mere invincibility and all-enduring valour, saved Wellington from failure in that great fight.'

By now Bonaparte had abdicated, and the long wars were over. At least that was the theory at the time. The Battalions came home, the 1st to Ireland, and the skeleton cadre of the 2nd to Aberdeen, where it was disbanded.

A year later Napoleon escaped from Elba, and came back from the dead to the terror of the living. In the mad rush of the Hundred Days, the 42nd were shipped hastily

51

back to Flanders. The Highlanders were particular favourites of the citizens of Brussels, where they were billeted. Their hosts said that they were alarmed that men so humane and gentle would be no match for Napoleon's fierce warriors. 'Those charming men with petticoats, who, when billeted on the inhabitants, helped to make the soup and rock the cradle for the half-frightened mistress of the family.'

On June 15 the Black Watch performed reels and sword-dances at the Duchess of Richmond's Waterloo Ball. That night a fashionable lady wrote in her diary: 'At four o'clock in the morning I went to the window (it was the finest morning possible). I saw the Highland Regiments march-ing out to the tune of "Hieland Laddie".' Many of the Black Watch officers who had been at the ball were still in their white dress knee-breeches.

After a long slog in full marching order, the Black Watch arrived at Quatre Bras cross-roads just after 3 p.m. And they were immediately locked in a 5-hour battle which pinned down Marshal Ney from going to Napoleon's help at Ligny. In this way the impromptu battle sealed Bona-parte's fate, by preventing him from wiping out Blücher, old 'Forwärtz', at Ligny before the British and Prussian armies could join together.

The fields were deep with summer crops—'the stalks of rye were up to our bonnets'. The Black Watch were forming square in a field when they saw cavalry behind them. 'These are French lancers,' cried a Sergeant. 'No,' said his Commanding Officer, 'they belong to the Prince of Orange.' But the Sergeant had been a prisoner-of-war, and was sure they were French. And he was right. The skirmishers ran in with the cry: 'Square, Square, French cavalry.' But some of the lancers managed to get inside before the flank companies had time to complete the square. And there was a long, savage fight to root them out. A French officer, having had his horse shot from under him, was having the worst of a duel with a vast Black Watch Sergeant. 'Quarter, Quarter,' he shouted, the one word of English he knew. The Sergeant, whose English was nearly as minimal, shouted back: 'Och, Och, inteet, she's no going to put you in quarters at aal, at aal, put shust in twa halves, inteet'. Three successive Commanding Officers of the Regiment were killed or sorely wounded in a couple of minutes. Captain Archibald Menzies stood six feet six inches tall, without counting his feather bonnet, and commanded the Grenadier Company of the Regiment. He took on a flurry of lancers single-handed with his claymore, and killed many of them. Eventually he fell, punctured by 17 lance wounds. But as he fell he pulled a lancer off his horse on top of him, as a shield. And so, miraculously, he survived, and lived to a ripe old age. At dinner parties in Perthshire he used to entertain the company by claiming that of the 17 lance wounds he received, 14 were mortal.

After the Black Watch had disposed of the lancers, and still held on to Quatre Bras cross-roads, Ney hurled the cuirassiers, his heavy cavalry, on the British squares. He told their General: 'The safety of France is at stake. We must make a supreme effort. Take your cavalry, and fling yourself upon the British centre. Crush them. Ride them down.' A Black Watch Sergeant who was in the square wrote: 'Their heavy horses and steel armour seemed sufficient to bury us under them.' It was a day of hard pounding. But the Black Watch pounded longest. A French officer called out to them: 'Why don't you surrender? Surrender. You see you are beaten.' But they stood their ground until night-fall, when they were so reduced that they had to be formed into a single square with the next Battalion. The 42nd lost 298 men at Quatre Bras, and were again one of the four Regiments singled out for particular mention in Wellington's dispatch on the battle.

Perhaps because of their heavy casualties, the 42nd were

A prickly square of Royal Highlanders at La Haie Sainte, Waterloo, 1815.

not given a major role at the crowning carnage of Waterloo two days later. They held the line in the left centre of Wellington's position, just behind la Haye Sainte, against which Napoleon launched his first great infantry attack—13,000 bayonets, with the fire of 74 guns brushing a path before them like a broom of flame. Then the Black Watch opened their ranks to let the cavalry sweep down from behind the crest of that most Wellingtonian position, and shatter the tottering French Battalions. As the Scots Greys charged through the hedges which the Black Watch were lining, the Jocks cheered: 'Scotland for Ever'. The 42nd lost 5 killed and 45 wounded at Waterloo.

The 2nd Battalion of the 73rd (which was temporarily parted from the Black Watch at the time, and leading its own separate existence) was more heavily involved in the battle. They had as heavy casualties as the 42nd had had at Quatre Bras—only one officer out of 23 was left on his feet at the end of the tremendous day.

After the battle the wounded Highlanders returned to their kind hosts in Brussels. A Belgian lady describes meeting a Black Watch Private limping along, clinging on to some railings. She offered to help him. And he drew himself up, and said: 'I was born in Lochaber, and I do not care for a wound.' He then rather spoiled the effect by fainting at her feet.

The rest of the Regiment paraded in the grand victorious review of the Allies near Paris. The Emperor of Russia was much struck with the Highlanders. So a special private inspection of a Sergeant, a piper, and a private soldier was laid on for him. The Emperor gave them a most minute scrutiny, 'pinching them to see what they wore under the kilt', and apparently being highly delighted with the music of the pipes.

A visitor in Paris at the time writes: 'The Highlanders, on the whole, are the most martial-looking of the military varieties at Paris. They attracted the most attention, not only from the French, but from the Allies. And their high character was spoken of as much as their figures . . . their tartans, bonnets, and plumes were very much admired, and were imitated even by the ladies. . . . There was much

The army of occupation in Paris, 1815.

whispering and sniggering as they passed. And the fine ladies, as they eyed their short kilts through their lorgnons, confided their fears to each other in whispers: "My dear, if it should be windy".'

Chapter 4

AFTER SOME MONTHS in Paris in the army of occupation the Black Watch marched in November for Calais and home. It was a freezing winter, chattering with ice. The Highlanders had their flesh laid open and bleeding by the ruffling of their kilts against their knees. 'The icicles gathered in clusters at our eye-brows, and the whiskered men appeared as if they had been powdered by some hair-dresser'. There was a race to be first home, and when the transports came near the beach, some of the Highlanders jumped overboard, their kilts floating out on the water.

On the long march north, the 42nd was given a red hot reception wherever it stopped. Bells rang. Presents were showered. And 'every table smoked with savoury viands'. Their welcome to Edinburgh was ecstatic. A newspaper of the day describes the unprecedented excitement, flags, enthusiasm, glitter of bayonet and plume. 'The crowds were wedged together across the whole breadth of the street, and extended in length as far as the eye could reach; and this motley throng appeared to move like a solid body, slowly along, till the gallant Highlanders were safely lodged in the Castle'. Sir Walter Scott organized a sumptuous dinner for the Regiment in the Assembly Rooms. The return of the men to their barracks afterwards was a bit unsteady. But, writes one of the diners with a satisfied sigh: 'No lives were lost, though many a bonnet and kilt changed owners, and not a few disappeared entirely'.

In Edinburgh the Regiment was re-equipped with new

kilts, and assorted peace-time frills and finery. The old hands were disgusted by this new-fangled costume: 'The plaid now only consists of a yard and a quarter of tartan, a useless shred of cloth, like a child's pinafore reversed, and pinned to the back of the shoulder.'

In 1816 the Black Watch were sent hurriedly to Glasgow, apparently to break a strike—'one of those ebullitions of discontent and disaffection, so often manifested in large manufacturing towns'. In the next year, off to Ireland, where they spent the next eight years, keeping watch on the restless Irish as a police force; internal security, they call it nowadays. Like the original Highland Watch, the Black Watch were posted in tiny detachments all over the country. In 1825 they were ordered to Gibraltar, where they were stationed for seven years. Then to Malta, the sunny isles of Greece, and back to Edinburgh in 1836. Then on to Ireland, the Greek islands again, before returning to Malta in 1843.

During the long, roving years of peace, while military thinking ossified, the uniform of the Black Watch became peacock-elaborate. The men were dressed up in white leather pipeclayed gloves, buckles, spats, frills, gold lace, braid, a stock up to the ears, about six yards of garter on each leg—and other furbelows, including a bonnet that was 'a mountain of feathers'.

The kit was so intricate that the officers were unable to dress themselves without help. And for a time there was agitation in the Regiment against the kilt. The protests even found their way into the press. The complaints were about the hardness of the material of the kilt, and the expense to the men of providing their own hose. The real root of the trouble was that the officers seldom wore the kilt themselves, preferring tartan trews. So officers were ordered to wear the kilt for most duties, and the campaign against the traditional Highland dress died down.

The other gradual change in the quiet, complacent years

Black Watch uniform, 1841.

after Waterloo was that the 42nd, like the other Highland
Regiments, became much less exclusively 'Highland'. Up
until Waterloo Gaelic was spoken in the Black Watch
officers' mess. But the steady drain of depopulation from
the Highlands made it no longer possible to recruit from
the Highlands alone. Rich 'Southerners' from the Lowlands
were eager to become officers in the crack Highland
Regiments. There were more Lowlanders than Highlanders in the ranks. The old nick-name for a Highland
soldier of 'Donald' or 'Rory' died away, and was replaced
by 'Jock', which is basically a Lowland word. And the
customs and character of the old 'mountain' corps began
to change.

The change was resented by some of the old stagers. An

Englishman was gazetted Ensign in the Black Watch while it was in Malta. His reception was not enthusiastic. Eventually he was made 'to swallow a Scotch thistle', prickles and all, and wash it down with a Regimental glass of whisky. After which everyone shook hands with him as a brother Scotsman.

Now, after forty years' silence, the artillery roared in earnest again for the Crimean War—that muddled joint British and French expedition, 'forever memorable for the ferocious courage of the British troops, and the extraordinary incompetence displayed by the Generals on both sides'. In June 1854 the 42nd arrived in Scutari, in Turkey. A Highland Brigade was formed for the first time out of the Black Watch, the 79th (Cameron Highlanders), and the 93rd (Sutherland Highlanders, who are now one half of the Argyll and Sutherland Highlanders). The Brigadier was Sir Colin Campbell.

In September the allied armies invaded the Crimea. With bands playing, with ideas of war that were fifty years out of date, in their brilliant comic opera uniforms, they set out to march on Sebastopol sixty miles away. It was a savagely hot day. Men fell out in droves, tortured with thirst and cholera. The glittering, empty plain was littered with discarded shakos and mess tins. When at last in the afternoon they reached the first water, a stream called the Bulganek, the troops broke discipline and ranks. They rushed, pushing and scrambling, into the water knee-deep to drink—all except the Highland Brigade, who were held steady in their ranks by Sir Colin Campbell.

Later in the month the allied expedition marched into the Russian army, dug in on the precipitous far side of the river Alma. The steep, giant terraces should have been impregnable. Batteries of artillery and bristling redoubts brooded on the towering heights. The Russian commander was so sure that no sane man would attempt a direct assault on his position that he had invited along a picnic party of young ladies from Sebastopol to see the destruction of the allied armies. The girls were in ecstasies about the bright uniforms of the British.

And now, with the insanity which was a feature of the whole campaign, the British infantry were launched across the river, and up the bald, bloody slopes against superior numbers of infantry and entrenched artillery. The Light Infantry Division miraculously stormed the heights. But in the moment of triumph by mistake a bugle sounded 'Retire'. And, because they were not supported, the Light Division was driven down the hill again.

So the Guards and the Highland Brigade were formed up in a fragile line two miles wide and two men deep to march all the way up those fatal slopes again. Sir Colin Campbell addressed his Highlanders: 'Now men, the army will watch us; make me proud of the Highland Brigade'. He then rode to the front of the Black Watch, and gave the famous command which has become part of the legend of Scotland: 'Forward Forty-Second.'

Pipes wailed. The Russian guns whipped the Alma into a bloody foam, and tore great holes in the line. But the British marched on as steadily as if they were on parade; 'ceremoniously and with dignity,' wrote a spectator. Solid columns of Russian infantry were poured down the hill to meet them. Four Battalions of the Tzar's elite infantry came down on top of the Black Watch alone, 3,000 men against 830. But with a wild yell the Royal Highlanders broke them. The loose British formation allowed the soldiers room to aim. The unwieldy Russian columns were cramped. And the smashing Minié bullet of the new British rifle was far more lethal than the Russian musket.

A Russian officer wrote afterwards: 'This was the most extraordinary thing to us, as we had never before seen troops fight in lines of two deep, nor did we think it possible for men to be found with sufficient firmness of morale to be able to attack, in this apparently weak formation, our massive columns.' Nevertheless with a hectic dash the British drove the grey masses of Russian infantry from the heights of the Alma. The 42nd was the first Regiment to reach the top. The bass drummer of the Black Watch combined pleasure with business by capturing single-handed the bass drum of a Russian Regiment.

Sir Colin wrote home after the Alma: 'The men cheered very much. I told them I was going to ask the Commander-in-Chief a great favour—that he would permit me to have the honour of wearing the Highland bonnet during the rest of the campaign, which pleased them very much.' So a special bonnet was made for Sir Colin by six men of the Black Watch. The top third of its hackle was red, for the Royal Highlanders; the bottom two-thirds white, for the Cameron and the Sutherland Highlanders.

The 42nd were only lightly engaged at Balaclava, where their comrades, the Sutherlands, formed the famous thin red line tipped with steel. After the wild Russian winter

1855—The siege of Sebastopol.

of moaning wind and seeping mud and disease, the 42nd
went into the trenches besieging Sebastopol. In September
1855 an assault on the Great Redan, the key fort in the
Russian defences, failed. And the Highland Brigade was
moved up into the front line to try again the next day.
During the night a Sergeant of the Black Watch, surprised
by the sinister silence from the Redan, crept into it with a
patrol. It was empty. 'Nothing was heard but the heavy
breathing and groans of the wounded and dying, who,
with the dead, were the sole occupants of the massive
work'. The Russians had pulled out; had softly and suddenly vanished away. The war faltered dismally to an end
after another savage winter. During the campaign the
Black Watch lost 400 men, more than half through disease.
General Février proved a more deadly enemy than the
Russian commanders.

In a farewell speech to the Highland Brigade, Sir Colin
Campbell said: 'When you go home, as you gradually
fulfil your term of service, each to his family and his
cottage, you will tell the story of your immortal advance
in that victorious echelon up the heights of Alma, and may
speak of the old Brigadier, who led you, and who loved
you so well. The pipes will never sound near me without
carrying me back to those bright days when I was at your
head, and wore the bonnet you gained for me, and the
honourable decorations on my breast, many of which I
owe to your conduct. Brave soldiers, kind comrades, farewell'. In 1856 the Black Watch sailed home for garrison-
duty at Dover Castle. Queen Victoria reviewed them there,
and expressed herself 'highly satisfied' with the appearance
of the Regiment.

Next year the Indian Mutiny, long rumbling, erupted.
The 42nd sailed to Calcutta with many other British
Regiments to put it down. They found themselves under
command of their old leader from the Crimea, Sir Colin
Campbell. As soon as they arrived they made a remarkable

forced march of 78 miles in 56 hours to the relief of Cawn-pore—thirsty work in that climate. The extravagant Black Watch feathered bonnet was apparently just the thing for the mad-dog sun. The Highlanders suffered less from sun-stroke than troops in less exotic hats. 'It was also found to resist sword-cuts in a remarkable degree.'

Sir Colin's force added up to 5,000 infantry, 600 cavalry, and 35 guns, against a rather chaotic mob of 25,000 mutineers with 40 guns. The British routed them in a hand to hand fight at Cawnpore. The surprise was so sudden and complete that the Black Watch found chapatis still baking on the mutineers' fires, and bullocks still fastened to their carts. They chased the pathetic rabble 25 miles north to Serai Ghat, and finished them in another battle two days later. All but one of the rebels' guns were captured, as well as an enormous amount of other booty. The Grenadier Company of the Black Watch found a gong hidden in some straw at the bottom of a bullock cart. Ever since, this great gong has sounded the hours wherever the 42nd has been stationed.

In the spring of 1858 the Black Watch and the Suther-land Highlanders side by side stormed with bayonet into Lucknow, and swept the mutineers from their line of defences in front of the Bank House. Here Lieutenant Farquarson won the first of the eight Victoria Crosses which were awarded to men of the Black Watch during the Mutiny. This decoration had just been introduced, and was handed out perhaps a shade more liberally than it has been since. The Regiment was now part of a column which marched towards Bareilly to clear the province. Fifty miles north of Lucknow they came up against a fort called Rhooyah in dense jungle. The Rajah inside refused to surrender. No reconnaissance was made. Four companies of the Black Watch were ordered to attack the fort upon its only unassailable face.

After six hours of stubborn fighting the attack failed,

and the Highlanders drew back for the night; during which the mutineers slipped away out of the fort. A Quartermaster-Sergeant, a Lance-Corporal, and two privates of the Black Watch won Victoria Crosses in this inept engagement. After the withdrawal they ran back into the withering fire to rescue wounded soldiers, and the body of one of their officers, from the ditch right under the wall of the fort.

In May, while advancing on Bareilly, the column was attacked by a screaming horde of Ghazis, or Moslem fanatics. 'Brandishing their *tulwars*, with heads carried low covered by their shields, and uttering wild shouts of "Deen, Deen", they fell on with furious impetuosity'. They completely surrounded the 42nd. Sir Colin Campbell described the attack as 'the most determined effort he had seen during the war'. In a brief, bloody, hand-to-hand struggle the Highlanders annihilated their attackers with hot bayonets. The Colonel was pulled from his horse. He

Indian Mutiny. Colour-Sergeant William Gardener at Bareilly saves the life of his Colonel, kills three Ghazis with his bayonet, and wins the V.C. 1858.

E
65

was saved by one of his Colour-Sergeants, who bayoneted two of the rebels, and so won the V.C. The General was also wounded, 'and escaped with his life only by the promptitude with which the 42nd used the bayonet'.

In January of 1859 a detachment of the Black Watch under Captain John Lawson was guarding a river-crossing at Sissaya Ghat. His force of 37 men of F Company was surprised by 2,000 rebels who crossed the river at dawn. Lawson was desperately wounded early on. His Colour-Sergeant and all his N.C.O.s were killed. But two privates of the Regiment, Walter Cook and Duncan Millar, took command of the survivors. The handful of Highlanders held the enemy at bay all day from sunrise to sunset, and eventually drove them back over the river. The two privates were awarded Victoria Crosses, and the pipe tune 'Lawson's Men' still commemorates their long, brave day. Sir Colin Campbell described this action in a General Order as 'beyond all praise'. The Mutiny was finally extinguished in this year, and the Black Watch concentrated at Bareilly. Here, on New Year's Day in 1861 the Commander-in-Chief in India presented new colours to the Regiment. And the survivors of Lawson's Men were called out to the front of the parade, and commended. In July Queen Victoria officially authorised for the first time the Regiment's old Highland nickname, the Black Watch. But it went in brackets after the 42nd, Royal Highlanders. Not until 1922 did the Black Watch become the Regiment's chief name.

In 1868 the Regiment returned to Edinburgh, and spent the next five years in peaceful postings around Scotland and England. In 1873 the red hackle was off again to a new part of the globe—to the Gold Coast, in the expedition against Coffee, otherwise Kofi, Calcalli, 'the truculent king of Ashanti'. For this campaign the Highlanders handed their kilts and bonnets into store, and were issued with special kit of drab cloth and pith helmets. The Com-

mander of the expedition, Sir Garnet Wolseley, later Field
Marshal Viscount Wolseley, wrote in his memoirs: 'By
the middle of 1873 all the three British Battalions selected
for the campaign had reached the Gold Coast. All were
historic corps of great reputation, but the best of them
was the Black Watch.'

In 1874 they marched on Kumasi, the capital of the
Ashanti, 150 miles inland. The country was wild, and the
climate vile. The native carriers deserted en masse, and
the Black Watch volunteered to act as porters. On the road
to Kumasi they ran into a big ambush of Ashantis. Bullets
hummed out of the bush. Wolseley writes: 'For the honour
of breaking through the masses of enemy I selected my
best Battalion, the Black Watch.' 'To the astonishment of
all' the Colonel ordered 'Markers Out', and dressed the
Black Watch as if they were on parade in Perth. Then he
ordered: 'Pipes to the heads of Companies; the men will
cheer'. And the Companies wheeled off into the bush.
'The skirl of the pipes roused the Scotsmen to a fury, and,
like a disciplined avalanche, they rushed forward.'

Ambush after ambush was swept aside. And by evening
the column, led by the Black Watch with its pipers at its
head, tumbled triumphant into Kumasi. King Coffee fled
into the bush. H. M. Stanley, the roving American
journalist (the one who said on another occasion 'Dr.
Livingstone, I presume'), reported the campaign—'The
conduct of the 42nd on many fields has been belauded, but
mere laudation is not enough for this Regiment in action.
It was the audacious spirit and true military bearing on the
part of the Highlanders as they moved down the road to
Kumasi, which challenged admiration this day. Very many
were borne back seriously wounded, but the Regiment
never halted nor wavered; on it went, until the Ashantis,
perceiving it useless to fight against men who would
advance, heedless of ambuscades, rose from their coverts
and fled panic-stricken into Kumasi, being shot down

whenever they showed themselves to the hawk-eyed Scots. One man, Thomas Adams, exhibited himself eminently brave among these brave men: he led the way into Kumasi, keeping himself about ten yards ahead of his Regiment, bounding on the road like a well-trained hound on a hot scent.'

So by February the Gold Coast campaign was won, and the Black Watch returned to Portsmouth. Sergeant Samuel McGaw was given the Victoria Cross for his bravery on the expedition. And the following epic Regimental doggerel, which has various other versions, was sung for years afterwards.

'The rain may rain, and the snaw may snaw,
The wind may blaw, and the cock may craw,
But ye canna frichten Jock McGaw;
He's the stoutest man in the Forty-Twa.
The Ashantees,
When they saw the shanks of Jock McGaw,
They turned aboot, an' they fleed awa'.

In 1881 the Black Watch returned to Edinburgh, where it was re-united with an old, long-lost sister unit, the 73rd. Under the Territorial system introduced by the Cardwell reforms of that year, each Regiment in the infantry was to have two Battalions, one serving abroad and one at home, turn and turn about. The 'Highland' Regiments were also increased, at a time when there was a steady population drain from the Highlands. And the Regiments were each given their own recruiting area. The Black Watch, which had once recruited exclusively from all over the Highlands, was given for its area Fife, Forfar, and Perthshire, much of which was not in the Highlands at all. Traditionalists shook their heads.

Chapter 5

THE TIME HAS NOW COME to retrace the history of a tributary of the Black Watch, which broke away from the main stream of the Regiment a hundred years before. In 1881, after a century of circuitous wanderings around the trouble spots of the world, this independent branch 'The Old 73rd' was about to be re-united with its parent Regiment.

It was raised in 1779 as a 2nd Battalion of the Royal Highland Regiment, which was away fighting George Washington and his rebellious united colonies in America. Eight officers were detached from the 1st Battalion to form the back-bone of the 2nd. This was a year of crisis for Britain. She was at war with Spain and France. Across the Atlantic there were the rebellious colonies. In India the prince of mighty Mysore, Hyder Ali, had renewed his war against us, helped by French military advisers. Russia, Sweden, and Norway had just organized an 'Armed Neutrality' in Europe directed against Britain. And in 1780, Britain herself declared war on Holland for aiding the Americans.

So, to supply the men to fight all these wars on different fronts, right and left around the country 2nd Battalions were hastily raised. This was when the *Scots Magazine* in fulsome capitals and rolling prose appealed to all north Britons, but chiefly Highlanders ('uncorrupted by the universal depravity of your southern countrymen') to repair to the drumhead of the new 2nd Battalion of the 42nd, which was now raising.

The new Battalion was embodied in Perth in 1780. The next year it set off on an expedition to take possession of the Cape of Good Hope. But the French arrived there first after a fierce race. So the 2nd Battalion was diverted to India, where it arrived in bits and pieces, having been scattered by naval actions, and by wayward winds. The voyage took 13 months in all, and 121 Highlanders died of fever and scurvy.

The 2nd Battalion's first action was at Panianee, on the south-west coast of India in 1782. A small British force led by the Colonel of the Highlanders was attacked by a large Indian army under the French General Lally, and Tippoo Sahib, the son of Hyder Ali. The assault came in in four columns, but was repelled at all points. A single company of British did not hesitate to charge with the bayonet a column of whatever weight, without calculating numbers.

Hyder Ali died, and was succeeded by Tippoo. There is a letter from Colonel MacLeod of the Highlanders to Tippoo, explaining how grave a thing it is to accuse a Highlander of lying—Tippoo had apparently accused the Colonel of making a 'mensonge'. 'This is an irreparable affront. If you have courage enough to meet me, take a hundred of your bravest men on foot, meet me on the sea-shore, I will fight you, and the hundred men of mine will fight yours.'

But the war was not going well for Britain. Their Government in Bombay was incompetent and indecisive. Tippoo recaptured Bednore, the vast treasure town of Mysore. And in 1783 he advanced with an army of 100,000 Indians and French, with 90 guns, against Mangalore on the west coast. The British garrison consisted of the 2nd Battalion of the Black Watch (500 men), plus 1,500 Sepoys, all under Major John Campbell of the Highlanders. Tippoo hoped that Mangalore would be petrified into surrender. He was disconcerted when the Black Watch attacked his

70

advance guard on a sortie 12 miles from Mangalore, and captured all its guns.

Tippoo now laid professional siege to the town, advised by the French experts. The walls of the fortress were breached and reduced to ruins. There was daily hand-to-hand fighting in the rubble. But the garrison held out for nine months of slow starvation, and trickery, and mining. They were driven to eating their horses and dogs, frogs and crows. Several feeble attempts to relieve them failed. The Highlanders became so fond of the Sepoys fighting with them, that they adopted 'these brave blacks' into their own Regiment, and renamed them the 3rd Battalion of the Royal Highland Regiment.

Eventually Tippoo offered honourable terms, and the handful of gallant men surrendered, and marched out with flags flying and all the honours of war. They had been reduced to half their original number, and were hardly able to stand, threadbare with starvation and disease.

Tippoo presented Major Campbell with an Arab charger and a sabre, in admiration for the stubborn gallantry of the defence. Mangalore was added to the battle honours of the Black Watch, even though technically it was a defeat. And a historian of the British army called the defence of the fortress 'as noble an example as any in history'.

A bizarre Regimental character of the period was one John Oswald, the son of an Edinburgh goldsmith. Oswald bought a commission in the 42nd, and then transferred to the 2nd Battalion in India. Out there he 'adopted the habits of a Hindu, and refrained from animal food'. He became Adjutant, but his behaviour was so tyrannical and eccentric that he was removed from his position and left the army. He was an ardent republican, and joined the French army when the Revolution broke out. He was killed in action commanding a French Regiment in which two of his sons were drummers.

When the Treaty of Versailles brought an uneasy peace

to the world, most 2nd Battalions were disbanded. But representations were made about the fine record of the Highlanders in India. And it was decided that the 2nd Battalion of the Black Watch should be formed into a separate unit to be called the 73rd Highland Regiment. The change was made in Bengal in 1786. For a time the 73rd continued to wear the Black Watch uniform, though the facings were altered from the blue of a Royal Regiment to green.

In 1787 a young Ensign called Arthur Wellesley, who would one day be the Duke of Wellington, obtained his first commission in the 73rd, and put on the kilt. The 73rd spent the years of fragile peace in India; in Cawnpore, Calcutta, and on the Madras coast. In the winter of 1792 the 73rd was part of the army which stormed Tippoo Sahib's stronghold of Seringapatam in a brilliant night attack. Under a fitful moon the Regiment waded across 500 yards of river, over which the musket flashes seemed one continuous flame; they cleared the fortifications with the bayonet, and almost caught Tippoo himself in his tent.

The Old 73rd, originally the 2nd Bn. The Black Watch at Seringapatam, 1792.

The 73rd storm Tippoo Sahib's stronghold of Seringapatam.

In the treaty after this battle Tippoo had to surrender half his kingdom. The 73rd next assisted at the capture of Pondicherry in 1793. From 1795–97 they fought in Ceylon. In 1799 they took part in the final campaign which disposed of the unfortunate Tippoo Sahib permanently. The army charged irresistibly into Seringapatam. Tippoo's ceremonial staff was captured as loot by the 73rd, and today decorates the Black Watch Regimental museum in Balhousie Castle, Perth.

As the Regimental Ballad of the Old 73rd puts it, without much modesty:

'Great Mars, the God of War, did never see such men before,
Nor Alexander fight like us at Mangalore.
At Seringapatam we fought, and Tippoo Sahib we slew;
'Twas there we showed the black dogs what the 73rd could do.'

In 1806 the Regiment returned to Scotland. Recruiting was dismally difficult, and the ranks of the Regiment were opened to English and Irish. In 1809 the 73rd was ordered, after much protest, to give up the Highland dress. And for the next 50 years it ceased to be officially either a Highland

73

or a kilted Regiment. In this year too the 73rd Regiment raised its own 2nd Battalion, just to confuse matters. This 2nd Battalion of the 73rd had a short, exotic life. In 1813 it went to Swedish Pomerania to join an allied expedition against Bonaparte. After forced marches across Germany averaging 30 miles a day, it arrived at Gorde near Hanover in the nick of time to turn the battle against the French. It was the only British Regiment engaged in the battle. There is evidence from this campaign that the heart of the Regiment was still Highland. A Sergeant of the 2nd Battalion of the 73rd wrote after Gorde: 'During our forced marches through Germany the most serviceable man we had was our old piper, Hugh Mackay; who when men were tired and straggling would fall back to the rear, and striking up some lively air he would soon have the whole Regiment about him like a cluster of bees. He would often go among the country people playing his pipes to the delight of the inhabitants with whom he was an especial favourite.'

This Battalion was stationed 12 miles south of Waterloo when Napoleon escaped from Elba. It had 53 casualties at Quatre Bras. At Waterloo it was in the right centre of the line in Halkett's Brigade, where the desperate French cavalry charges crashed most fiercely. Wellington himself took refuge inside the square of his old Regiment during the hottest part of the action. The 73rd was charged 11 times by cavalry, and hammered by artillery at point-blank range. Its standard was prudently sent to the rear to keep it out of harm's way. But the British infantry squares, bristling with triple rows of bayonets, stood firm, and the centre of the line held, just. Wellington was heard to murmur: 'Night or the Prussians must arrive'.

The 73rd had 330 casualties, and ended up being commanded by its only surviving officer, a junior Lieutenant. As the old boastful ballad puts it:

'A troop of the French cavalry came bravely charging down,
We were ordered to form solid square, and quickly it was done;
But when their Colonel came in sight our numbers for to see,
He quickly cried 'Retraite Mes Braves, for them's the Seven
and Three.'

In this way the Black Watch was the only British
Regiment with two of its Battalions at Waterloo. After
the battle the 2nd Battalion was disbanded, but many of its
men were absorbed into the 1st Battalion.

On the other side of the world this 1st Battalion of the
73rd had been putting down a miniature revolution in
Australia. The Governor of Botany Bay was William
Bligh; the one who made his notorious name at the mutiny
on the Bounty. As Governor, apparently, he was 'so
tyrannical, arbitrary and capricious that it is only charitable
to suppose he was mad'.

The unfortunate inhabitants petitioned the Commanding
Officer of the troops in Sydney to put Bligh under arrest,
and proclaim martial law. This he did, with alacrity.
Britain was not amused. And at the end of 1809, after a
voyage of more than six months, the 1st Battalion of the
73rd and two Men-of-War arrived at Sydney to restore
the King's representative. The orders of the Commanding
Officer of the 73rd were to release Bligh and reinstate him
for 24 hours as a gesture. He was then to take Bligh's place
as Governor of Botany Bay. The unhappy military commander of the colony who had arrested Bligh was sent
home under strict arrest. There he was found guilty of
mutiny, and cashiered. The Highlanders spent the next
four years in Australia, hunting down bush-rangers and
jolly swagmen in the wild out-back.

In 1814 they were posted to Ceylon, to garrison the
island against the possibility of a French invasion. In the
autumn there was trouble in Kandy. The King of Kandy
ruled over the 60 mile square of tangled mountains and
jungle in the centre of the island. In October he seized ten

British subjects, and cut off their noses, their right ears, and their right arms. The assorted bits and pieces were tied around their necks, and they were sent back over the frontier, *pour encourager les autres*, and as an awful warning of the hazards of trespassing on Kandy's territory.

Britain declared war. And in 1815 the 73rd and other Regiments marched up into the wild, unhealthy interior, where the spicy breezes blew soft with disease, and dysentery, and danger. The going was so rough that the troops were broken up into miniature columns of between 70 to 250 men. Each column had its little train of artillery, and its native soldiers. The King ran away into the bush, but he was later given up to the British. His crown, sceptre and throne were sent home to become part of the furniture of Windsor Castle.

But there was still trouble in the mountains. Pretenders and new kings laid claim to the vanished throne of Kandy. Invisible deadly hands in the jungle fired arrows, and then slipped away. The 73rd were scattered around in small detachments to keep the peace. In 1818 four men of the Regiment and 12 men of the native Ceylon Regiment, commanded by Lance-Corporal McLaughlan of the 73rd, were ambushed in dense jungle by a large body of Kandyans. Two men of the 73rd were shot dead at once. The Lance-Corporal left nine men to stand over their bodies, and fought his way with the other five to Badulla, 50 miles south-east of Kandy. When he returned with reinforcements two hours later, he found the nine still fighting furiously, still standing firm where he had left them. Special medals were struck for the Lance-Corporal and three of his men. Later the sacred tooth of Buddha was captured from the rebels by an Ensign of the 73rd, and this took the steam out of the rebellion.

In 1821 the 73rd returned to Britain, and for the next 30 years served in scattered stations all round the world—in Scotland, Ireland, Gibraltar, and the Channel Islands. In

1838 the Regiment sailed to Canada, and fought against Canadian nationalists supported by American irregulars from across the border. In 1845 the 73rd sailed from Cork for South Africa. But it was diverted en route to Rio de Janeiro, and then into Montevideo where an unheroic, incomprehensible siege was in process. Britain was meddling on behalf of the 'Unitarios' of Argentine against a Federal Army under the bloody dictator Rosas, whose trading policy she didn't like. The 73rd was sent into Montevideo to help the garrison. The siege had many elements of musical comedy including Giuseppe Garibaldi and a group of Italian volunteers who were acting as pirates. The besieging Federal army made no effort to get into the city, which it could have taken easily. Eventually, after seven months' siege, Britain became sick of the adventure, and the 73rd sailed on to South Africa.

En route they were tempest-tossed by a terrible gale, and their high-flying former Ensign, now the Duke of Wellington and Commander-in-Chief of the army, commended their coolness under storm in a special General Order. In South Africa the Regiment fought in three Kaffir Wars in rapid succession, rounding up tens of thousands of head of cattle like cowboys, storming into kraals, scouring the big country, ambushing and being ambushed.

In the second of these incoherent 'wars' four officers of the 73rd on patrol together were cut off and killed. The Xosas developed a new tactic which nonplussed the British. When the 73rd approached, they sat down on the ground and ignored them. Clothes fell to rags after a few days of patrol in the bush. The hooked thorns of the 'wait-a-bit' ripped at everything. The officers hardly made any pretence of wearing uniform. The ridiculous coatees and useless shakos of the men were replaced by big peaked caps and grey jackets. The 73rd was stationed out on the frontier for years, if there can be a 'frontier' in a war where the enemy was everywhere, in the front, flanks, in the rear,

77

and even occasionally under the water with only his nose showing.

In 1852, during these Kaffir wars, the steam troop-ship *Birkenhead* carrying drafts for all the Regiments in South Africa struck a pinnacle rock off Danger Point near Cape Town. The ship stuck fast, and broke in two. It was black of night, and dead calm. The women and children were put into the boats. But there was no room for all the troops. So these young soldiers of the new drafts stood firm in their ranks on the deck—'biding God's pleasure and their chief's command, went down erect, defiant, to their grave beneath the sea'. More than 350 men were drowned, 56 from the 73rd, more than from any other Regiment.

One officer who survived wrote that the behaviour of all ranks 'far exceeded anything that I thought could be effected by the most perfect discipline . . . all received and carried out their orders as if embarking for a world's port in lieu of eternity. There was only this difference, that I never saw any embarkation conducted with so little confusion'.

The *Birkenhead* left a deep mark on the British army, and on people's attitudes to disaster at sea, and the doctrine of 'women and children first'. In almost his last public speech the Duke of Wellington surprised some of his audience by saying nothing about the courage and devotion of the troops, but returning again and again to their discipline. The King of Prussia ordered the story of the *Birkenhead* to be read out at the head of every one of his Regiments as an example of perfect military obedience.

In 1852 the 73rd, still fighting the Kaffirs, were scouring an inaccessible mass of mountains. The Regiment stormed a famous stronghold in the cliffs known as Macomo's Den, which was supposed to be impregnable. The only approach was down a great flight of natural steps. A female prisoner acted as their guide into the den. Four guns fired shells into the cleft, and then the Regiment charged in. Over 100 women and children were taken unhurt from among the crannies of the cave. And in the campaign 6,000 Kaffir warriors, 80 chiefs, 80,000 cattle, 'besides goats innumerable' were captured.

In 1858 the 73rd was posted to India, and arrived in time to perform in the closing scenes of the Mutiny or, as the Indians prefer to call it, 'The First War of Independence'. It returned to Britain in 1861, and the next year, in acknowledgement of its origin, it was given the title of the 73rd Perthshire Regiment. The next years took the 73rd to Ireland, Hong Kong, Ceylon, and India. In 1881 the old Regiment paraded in Portsmouth for the last time. It was about to be reunited with its parent Regiment, the 42nd, from which it had sprung fully armed a century before. The Cardwell reforms of this year meant that every Regiment was to have two Battalions, each serving alternately at home and abroad. As the 73rd marched past the Commander-in-Chief of the army for the last time, the Roman numerals LXXIII of the Regimental colour fell to the ground. They had been rusted away by years of roaming and fighting around the wild forgotten places of the world.

Chapter 6

IN 1882 THE 1ST BATTALION of the Black Watch
sailed to Egypt in an expedition against Arabi Pasha.
Arabi was the son of a peasant family. He was con-
scripted into the Egyptian army, and rose from the ranks
to become first a Colonel, and then Minister of War. He
called himself 'the Egyptian', and was the leader of the first
fierce stirrings of Egyptian nationalism against Turkish
and western European imperialism. The British were
alarmed at Arabi's growing influence, so they sent a fleet
to Alexandria to discourage him. Riot blazed in the streets
of Alexandria and Cairo, killing many Europeans. Arabi
took command of the rebel mobs. In September the British
expedition under Sir Garnet Wolseley landed at Ismalia
to restore the *pax Britannica*. Arabi, with a bigger army,
was entrenched at Tel-el-Kebir. The British made a long
night march and stormed Arabi's entrenchments with the
bayonet just before dawn. The Highland Brigade with
the Black Watch led the attack, and bore the brunt of the
assault. By 6.30 a.m. the battle was over, and the Egyptians
had been overwhelmed, with very heavy casualties. The
Black Watch lost about 50 killed and wounded. They then
marched into Cairo with the army of occupation. Arabi
surrendered, and was exiled to Ceylon. Apparently,
'though not a great leader, and certainly no soldier, his
popularity rested on his simple kindly disposition'.

This victory and others like it, had an unfortunate effect
on British military thinking. The Generals were encouraged to put their trust in night marches and frontal

Tamai, 1884. The Fuzzy-Wuzzies break a British square. The Black Watch form the nearest side of the nearest square.

assaults, which were successful against Arabi's unmilitary mob. These tactics proved catastrophic on occasions in the Boer War against opponents who could sit firm and shoot straight.

The next two years were spent in detachments around Egypt, where there was an epidemic of cholera. In the spring of 1884 the Black Watch marched in an expedition against the wild and restive tribesmen of the hilly country of eastern Sudan, whom Kipling christened Fuzzy-Wuzzies—' 'E's the only thing that doesn't give a damn for a Regiment of British Infantree'. The Highlanders were caught in the thick of a fierce battle at El Teb while they were marching to the relief of an isolated British garrison. They attacked a superior force of dervishes, and after five hours of severe fighting, totally defeated them. In the next month they fought at Tamai, where the frenzied and fanatic Fuzzy-Wuzzies broke a British square. The British fought in two squares, and the Brigadier allowed a gap to form in the square of which the Black

Watch was one side. The Fuzzy-Wuzzies broke in and captured the naval guns. But after a hot fight, they were chased out, and the guns were recovered. Private Thomas Edwards of the Black Watch won the Victoria Cross for bringing in the body of a dead naval officer and a machine gun which was about to be carried away.

Perhaps it is from Tamai that the scurrilous myth about the spats of the Black Watch sprang. The *canard*, for which there seems to be no evidence, is spread, particularly by Welsh Regiments. It runs that the Black Watch (or sometimes one of the other Highland Regiments) wear the toes of their white spats cut straight across as a deep disgrace for breaking the square on some rather nebulous occasion. In 1914, if a private from another Regiment felt like starting a fight, he would go into a bar where men of the Black Watch were drinking, and ask not for 'pig's ear', which is rhyming slang for beer, but for a pint of 'broken square'. Then belts would be unbuckled. It can't have been the Black Watch at Tamai, anyway. For one thing the hole in the square was caused by bad orders, not by cowardice. For another, the hole was rapidly repaired and the damage undone. And for another, the old prints show the Black Watch wearing square toes to their spats long before 1884.

The Black Watch lost 60 killed and 29 wounded in this battle, about half of the total British casualties. More than 2,000 dervishes were killed. In the Sudan campaigns the Highlanders wore pith helmet topees, with the inevitable red hackle on the side. After the victory at Tamai, they returned to Cairo.

But in the autumn they were off to the Sudan again to fight against Mohammed Ahmed Ibn Seyyid 'Abdullah, better known as the Mahdi. Mohammed said that one of his descendants, to be called Al-Mahdi 'the divinely directed one', would come one day as an Imam of God, to fill the earth with equity and justice—and incidentally kill all the unbelievers. In 1881 Mohammed Ahmed, the son of a boat-builder on the Nile, announced that he was the Mahdi, and called a holy war against the corrupt Egyptian rulers of the Sudan.

By 1884 he had made himself master of most of the Sudan; except for Khartoum, where General Gordon still held out with his small garrison. So the Black Watch set off up the Nile in the river column to relieve Khartoum. At Dongola, the Mahdi's birth-place, one of the whale-boats was swamped, and a Major drowned. In February 1885, further up the Nile and getting near to Khartoum, the Black Watch were part of a British force of 1,000 who stormed the heights of Kirbekan, which were held by a strong force of the Mahdi's men. 'The pipers struck up, and with a cheer the Black Watch moved forward with a steadiness and valour which the enemy was unable to resist, and which called forth the admiration of the General . . . . Without a check the Battalion advanced, scaled the rocks, and drove the enemy from their shelters'. Meanwhile, the cavalry had gone round behind, and captured the enemy's camp. The British General was killed during the assault. The Black Watch fought again at Abu Klea, and then came the news that the other relieving column had arrived, two days too late. Khartoum had fallen. Gordon was dead. The river column turned round, and went back down-stream to Cairo. In 1886 the Battalion moved to Malta; in 1889 to Gibraltar. In 1893 it split in two, with half the Battalion going to Cape Town, and the other half to Mauritius. The half in South Africa sent out a small expedition to put down some unpleasantness in Matabele-land. In 1896 the two halves came together again, and sailed for India for five years' garrison duty.

Meanwhile, the 2nd Battalion, whose turn it was for home service, had spent the last 20 years in sundry stations in Scotland, England, and Ireland. In the 1880s they were used to suppress some unhappy Irish disturbances. Then

Preparations for New Year's Day in the 1890's.

in October 1899 Paul Kruger, 'Oom Paul' (Uncle Paul), the heavily whiskered President of the Transvaal declared independence from British suzerainty. And the Boer War, to settle whether the Boers and Afrikaners or the British were going to control the bottom end of Africa, and to shatter the complacent British illusion about the invincibility of their army, erupted.

It was not a happy war for the British infantry—foot-slogging over Africa with unwieldly mule and ox-wagon trains, while the mounted infantry of the Boer burghers rode rings round them, and picked them off at long range with their Mauser carbines. The 2nd Battalion of the Black Watch was one of the first units from Britain to arrive in South Africa. It joined the Highland Brigade, commanded by Major-General 'Andy' Wauchope, a famous Black Watch character. He was also known as 'Red Mick', and had been wounded with the Regiment twice in Ashanti, once at El Teb, and once at Kirbekan. The Highland Brigade was part of a column marching to relieve Kimberley, the Diamond City, where Cecil Rhodes was complaining furiously about being beleaguered. A force of

8,000 Boers blocked their way at a rocky kopje called Magersfontein. It rose 200 feet out of the plain, and was the key to the door of Kimberley. The Boers secretly dug a line of trenches at the foot of this hill, and waited. The British decided to make a five mile march on the position at night, and attack at first dawn. The Black Watch and the rest of the Highland Brigade were to be the first wave of the assault. Wauchope was not enthusiastic about the idea of a night march, but he refused to argue about his orders. The Highlanders marched half an hour after midnight. It was a black night, lit only by flashes of lightning, and the beams of the searchlights of the Diamond City beyond the hill—'one of those nights in which one literally cannot see one's hand'. Thunderstorm rolled like an ominous Wagnerian overture.

The downpour turned the sandy veldt into a morass, and the ground was littered with prickly clumps of mimosa and boulders. It was nightmare country for a night movement. The troops had to march in the closest possible formation so as not to lose touch with each other. So they moved in 'mass of quarter-columns', each company being drawn up shoulder to shoulder in two lines, with a third line of supernumeraries. They were boxed in by ropes held by guides on either flank. The result was that the Highland Brigade, 4,000 men in an immense rectangle of 96 close order lines, struggled through the filthy night more slowly than expected in the plan. At 4 a.m. Magersfontein loomed out of the first streak of dawn half a mile ahead. This was supposed to be a surprise attack. But the effect had been slightly spoiled by the fact that the British had bombarded the kopje with their artillery for two hours on the previous evening. As soon as the barrage stopped the Boers had filled their trenches in expectation of a dawn attack. The British, having not bothered to reconnoitre, had no suspicion that the Boers were tightly entrenched at the foot of the hills. So just as the Highlanders started

Magersfontein, 1899. The Black Watch are cut to pieces at dawn.

to deploy from their dense formation there came a tremendous fusillade at point blank range, the biggest roar of musketry that anyone there had ever heard. A hail of bullets poured into the serried ranks of the Highland Brigade, not from the hill where they had expected the Boers to be, but from the hidden trenches under their very feet. Not for the first, nor for the last time in the war, the British had walked straight into a Boer trap.

Black Watch men have always been incorrigible writers of verse about battles, and camp-fires, and nostalgia for the Highlands. A Black Watch private who was at Magersfontein wrote—

> 'Tell you the tale of the battle, well, there's not much
>   to tell;
> Nine hundred men went to the slaughter, and nigh four
>   hundred fell.
> Wire, and Mauser rifle, thirst, and a burning sun
> Knocked us down by hundreds ere the day was done.'

Another bitter Highlander complained that the Brigade

had 'been led into a butcher's shop, and bloody well left there'.

Wauchope was shot dead as he walked coolly forward to inspect the position. The Highlanders fell on their faces in chaos, 200 yards from the Boer trenches, scrambling for cover behind the mimosa bushes. And there they lay for most of the day, beneath the savage sun. They had no food. Water bottles were soon empty. The sun cooked great blisters on the backs of their knees, which were unprotected by their kilts. Even those who were not hit were out of action for several days. Of the 943 men of the Black Watch who walked into the massacre, 301 were killed or wounded. Of the 27 officers, 17, including the C.O., were casualties. A small party of Black Watch and Seaforths made a plucky but ultimately unsuccessful attempt to climb the right side of the hill, and take the Boer trenches in the rear. It was a black week for Britain, where it was a freezing, foggy December. In Edinburgh all dances were cancelled. Princes Street suddenly seemed to be full of women in mourning.

In February the Highlanders seized Koodoosberg Drift on the road to Kimberley. Later in the month they caught up with the Boer army under bearded Piet Cronje at Paardeburg Drift on the Modder River. The Boers took cover behind the natural fortress of the river bank. In spite of recent experiences, Kitchener decided again on a full-scale frontal assault across the river on the Boer position. And again the Highlanders were chosen for the job. They marched in extended line across a mile of open country upon the river. The line grew thinner and thinner; and thicker and thicker the khaki patches on the grass behind it. The General of the next door Division wrote in his memoirs: 'I never hope to see or read of anything grander than the advance of that thin line of Highlanders across the coverless plain, under a hail of lead from their invisible enemy in the river-banks'. But the frontal assault not surprisingly wavered to a standstill. The Black Watch and the Seaforths got nearer to the Boer Laager than any other units and actually crossed the river just downstream from their enemy. The attack was a tactical failure. It did not over-run the Boer position. But at least it trapped them by destroying their horses and trek oxen. For a week after the first assault the British pounded the Boer position with lyddite and shrapnel. The Modder was foul with swollen carcases of horses and cattle, and cholera and enteric fever broke out in the British army, who drank the water regardless. After ten days Cronje surrendered with his 4,000 men. And Paardeburg was written among the battle honours of the Black Watch for their brave but hopeless advance across the naked plain.

In March the column was marching up the Modder on Bloemfontein. The Boers made a stand at Poplar Grove. After a few hours of desultory fighting the Highlanders cleared them from their trenches. The Boers left so hurriedly that their cooking pots were still boiling on the fires, and most of the Black Watch 'got a rather comforting drink of hot coffee'. But the action was a disappointment. The cavalry were supposed to swing round and cut off the Boers' retreat. But they were too late. And the commando got clean away. The Boers were now, in their General De Wet's own words 'a disorderly crowd of terrified men flying before the enemy'. And later in the month the Black Watch marched into Bloemfontein, and the Union Jack floated over the brick and tin capital of the Orange Free State. The Highland Brigade next marched in a great column north up the railway on Pretoria. At Sannah's Post they were too late to reinforce some harassed cavalry. At Babiaansberg, 'Baboon Mountain', the Black Watch stormed a sheer table mountain with bullets rattling down the 'kloof' around their ears. They marched 380 miles in 37 days to reach Pretoria. These were months of long frustrating marching after a gad-fly enemy. The Black Watch were issued with soft felt slouch hats worn by the Boers instead of their worn-out helmets. So the red hackle was worn on yet another new style of head-gear. 'Boer above and bare below' someone described the Highlanders.

In July the Black Watch marched 34 miles in $15\frac{1}{2}$ hours. During the operations about Retief's Neck, five companies of the Black Watch carried a strong position in fine style, with the loss of two officers and 17 men. They were then split up into detachments to man the blockhouses which were intended to net the elusive Boer commandos. Kitchener's desperate new plan for finishing the embarrassing war was to carve up the country with chains of blockhouses, linked by barbed wire entanglements. He built 8,000 blockhouses, usually between a mile and a half mile apart, covering a distance of 4,000 miles. The Black Watch manned these blockhouses around Harrisburg in the Orange Free State in detachments varying from six to 30 men. The idea was to stop the Boer guerrillas from crossing and re-crossing the country as they wished. They could now only break through the barbed wire barricades at night, and at some hazard. The Black Watch took part in various drives by British columns to mop up the roving commandos in the space between the blockhouse chains. In December 1901 the 1st Battalion landed in Durban to participate in the closing, bitter end of the war; it was stationed beside the 2nd Battalion at Harrisburg for blockhouse duty and railway guarding. A young Second Lieutenant had just joined the 2nd Battalion. His father had commanded the Battalion. The son was to become one of the great Black Watch soldiers and Field Marshals. His name was A. P. Wavell.

Perhaps there were lessons that could have been learned from the Boer War—lessons about barbed wire, and the fire-power of modern weapons; hints that in a future war the defence might have a built-in advantage over the attack; implications that the old-fashioned frontal infantry

89

assault, advancing shoulder to shoulder with bayonets fixed, had become not so much out of date, more a quick way of committing suicide. There was a terrible lesson lurking somewhere that the nature of war itself was changing. Since the Goths came swarming down from the hill, fighting had been a business of seasonal manœuvring by professional armies, brutal and bloody, but usually regulated by rules of the game. In the Boer War there were indications, for anyone who cared to read them, that war might be about to escape from its cage, omnivorous, insatiable, involving civilians as well as the professionals, and no longer a possible way of settling anything.

These are not the sort of lessons however which an infantry Battalion is paid to learn, even a Battalion which contains a budding military genius like Wavell's. The Black Watch Battalions returned to the orderly routine of peace-time soldiering, to mess nights and field days. At the Delhi Durbar in 1911 the 2nd Battalion was, predictably, congratulated on its magnificent turn-out by King George V—Royalty, since Victoria, has always been enthusiastic about the kilt, sometimes to the irritation of trousered Regiments. The 1st Battalion spent the first years of the new century, the last years of the old world, in home postings. In 1914, when earth's foundations fled, it was at Aldershot as part of the 1st Guards Brigade of the 1st Division. This has been described as 'one of the finest Brigades ever to take the field'—but the field had changed into something totally strange, terribly unlike the field days around Aldershot.

In one way at least the army was ready for the descending avalanche. In 1908 Lord Haldane organized the Territorial Army, and various militia units from Perthshire, Fife, and Angus, with long links with the Regiment, formally became Battalions of the proliferating Black Watch. There was soon to be room for them all, and for many more civilian-soldiers, in the trenches of Flanders.

Chapter 7

To follow the black watch through the mud, and blood, and muddle of the 1914–18 war is almost as confusing a business as the real thing must have been. A fifth horseman called 'Chaos' joined the Four Riders of the Apocalypse. The reader, like the Highlanders of 1916, is soon lost in the convoluted labyrinth of trenches, saps, and mines, waist-deep in liquid mud, in which units were broken into fragments, and whole companies vanished without trace. Month-long battle merged into month-long battle, and shell-hole overlapped shell-hole. Subalterns found themselves commanding Battalions. And the Commanding Officers of neighbouring and shattered Battalions of the 'Watch' bumped into each other, together in a dug-out, two men peering up over the edge to fire desperate rifles at the tidal wave of grey-coated German infantry. All one can hope to do is to catch an occasional glimpse of the red hackle through the murk and the mist. Pipers lead a line of Highlanders over the top into the mincing machine-guns, playing something which is quite inaudible in the barrage, but which must be 'Highland Laddie'. The line of kilts covered with khaki aprons advances to impale itself on the enemy's wire entanglements. Names which still call back faintly the smoke and stir of the Great War constantly recur—Chocolat Menier Corner, Hill 70, Delville Wood, Longueval, and any number of 'Black Watch' corners and farms.

Some basic statistics are available. Twenty-five Battalions of the Black Watch served in the Great War. More than 50,000 men passed through the Regiment, of whom 8,000 were killed, and over 20,000 were wounded. Before 1914 the Black Watch had won 28 battle honours. During the 1914–18 war it gained another 69. Men of the Black Watch around the world won 9 Victoria Crosses. According to the story which all new recruits to the Regiment firmly believe, some German christened the Black Watch 'The Ladies from Hell'. Wherever the brazen throat of war bellowed loudest, the Highlanders were there.

But in spite of the butcher's arithmetic in the war diaries, the thing which surprises the reader so many years afterwards is the enthusiasm, at times even the gaiety of it all. Even in 1917 Battalions of the Black Watch are complaining bitterly and formally about being kept away from the killing ground of the Western Front. A Sergeant in the machine-gun section hangs out his kilt to dry, has it blown away by a shell, and soldiers on kiltless, to the recorded delight of his Battalion. Jocks bathe in the Tigris, dodging Turkish snipers' bullets. Then there is the livestock which the Black Watch acquire, and love through the black years—the reluctant pig of Beuvry; the old white horse 'Allez-vous-en', who earned three wound stripes, and was allowed to wear the red hackle; and the charger 'German Jimmy', captured from a patrol of Uhlans. Both horses were retired to Scotland at the end of the war.

A Lance-Corporal in the hungry trenches in Mesopotamia shoots a wild goose high on the wing with his rifle, and the whole Battalion blasts away in competition with him, but with less success. There are Highland gatherings, and Highland games, and piping, whenever two Battalions of the Black Watch pass in the night. There is even a wild boar hunt, beaters with fixed bayonets.

When war was declared, the 1st Battalion went straight into the cannon's opening roar from Aldershot, with the 1st Guards Brigade. The French civilians turned up en masse as they arrived to greet 'the famous Waterloo Black

Watch', and to collect glengarry badges. The small British Expeditionary Force was an appendix on the left, or north of the French line. On it the main enemy attack fell heaviest. The Germans hoped for a surprise encirclement of France from the north, a 'battle without a morrow', before the autumn leaves fell. The Black Watch fought all the way in the enforced and blind retreat from Mons, trudging long miles each day, 200 miles in a fortnight, on dusty roads under a blazing sun; turning all the time for desperate rear-guard fight; and hearing the French women cry 'Perfides' at them as they passed. At each ten minutes' halt on the march, everyone who was not on duty fell asleep. But the little regular army held the sky suspended until the Territorials and the New Army arrived.

On September 6 they turned at last at the river Marne, 50 miles short of Paris, and pushed into the gap which had been stretched between two of the German armies. The Germans retreated to the Aisne, where in a hot battle the 42nd lost its Commanding Officer and many others. But the battle without a morrow had disappeared without trace.

Now the Germans tried to break through in the north, to the Channel ports. And during November the 1st Battalion fought in the first battle of Ypres, helping to hold the thin, half-moon salient around the old Flemish city. In this wild, dogged race to the sea, the Battalion lost 29 officers and 478 other ranks. It also wiped out one of the crack Regiments of the Prussian Guard, who were advancing in mass formation singing 'Die Wacht am Rhein'. Its few survivors were captured after nightfall. In December Sir John French, the Commander-in-Chief, addressed the Battalion: 'You have suffered great losses . . . you have suffered great hardships . . . The Black Watch—a name we know so well—has always played a distinguished part in the battles of our country. I as Commander-in-Chief of this force thank you, but that is a small matter. Your country thanks you, and is proud of you.'

By now the 2nd Battalion had arrived in France from India, in the Indian Brigade with which it was to fight for the whole war. An impartial expert later in the war claimed that the best patrols in the British army were made up of mixed scouting parties of Black Watch and Pathans. The Pathans were unequalled at stalking invisibly up to an enemy trench. 'The Highlanders gave the necessary steadiness and feeling of security to the whole patrol'.

The 2nd Battalion found that the kilt was the best thing to wear in the quagmire of the winter of 1914. You could wade through trenches well over your knees, and arrive in comparative comfort, without wet cloth clinging to your legs. Highland shoes were less useful. They were sucked off by the glutinous mud. And the Highlanders stood for days, shivering in stockinged feet. So shoes were replaced by boots and puttees.

1915 on the Western Front was a depressing year of battering of heads against the German brick wall, and discovering that artillery was not much good at opening a path through barbed wire. It was a dark year of costly, disastrous attacks on the doubtful theory that steady attack at last wears down resistance. The French called it 'la guerre d'usure'. Both 1st and 2nd Battalions fought at Givenchy. And both again at the great battle of Festubert in May, in the unsuccessful British spring offensive. Here a Corporal of the 1st Battalion and a Corporal of the 2nd both won the V.C. within a mile of each other for heroic leading of their sections in the deadly breach. The 1st Battalion was the only one in its Division to reach the enemy trenches.

The Territorial Battalions, the 4th, 5th, 6th, and 7th had by now arrived in France. More than 60 per cent of the 7th Battalion were coal-miners from Fife, later to be much used in claustrophobic underground warfare, tunnelling like moles towards the enemy trenches. So six Battalions of the Black Watch were engaged at Festubert.

At Loos in September the British attacked the north of the wide salient now formed by the German lines in France. Both 1st and 2nd Battalions carried their objectives with heavy losses, disappearing into the cloud of green gas and sulphurous smoke, and finding the wire uncut. But they had to withdraw because the attack on either side had failed, and their flanks were exposed to the fresh German reserves, creeping in from the side with stick grenades. At Loos too the 'Service Battalions' of the new army joined the Regiment. The 8th Black Watch actually captured that place of death the Hohenzollern Redoubt, losing 19 officers and 492 other ranks. The 9th Black Watch attacked Loos itself and Hill 70, losing 21 officers and 680 other ranks— the heaviest losses ever suffered by any Battalion of the Regiment in one action. Of the 950 Highlanders who set out into the gas at dawn, only 98 came back a day later. An English General who visited the ground a few days after the battle wrote in his report: 'In front of the Lens Road Redoubt, the dead Highlanders, in Black Watch

Imperial War Museum

Royal Highlanders celebrate New Year's Day behind the trenches.

95

tartan, lay very thick. In one place, about 40 yards square, on the very crest of the ridge, and just in front of the enemy's wire, they were so close that it was difficult to step between them. Nevertheless the survivors had swept on and through the German lines. As I looked on the smashed and riven ground, I was amazed when I thought of the unconquerable, irresistible spirit which these men of the New Armies must possess, to enable them to continue their advance after sustaining such losses'.

The Highland Brigade of which the 9th Black Watch was part advanced four miles at Loos, and passed all but the last German trench lines. If they had had any reinforcements, the tactics of infiltration might have been introduced into the Western Front before they were, and the war of attrition shortened. After Loos the 2nd Battalion with its Indian division went to Mesopotamia.

In 1916 the 4th and 5th Territorial Battalions, which had been badly mauled, were amalgamated, and soldiered on, as they did after the war, as the 4th/5th Black Watch. In the summer of 1916 the main attack moved to the Somme, the strongest part of the German fortress line, in

A Black Watch piper leads Highlanders back after an attack at Longueval and Delville Wood in the Battle of the Somme, 1916.

order to lighten the pressure on the French further south at Verdun. Between July and October in the battle of the Somme the British lost 460,000 men, and discoloured the tawny ground of Picardy with their blood. Battalions of the Black Watch fought at High Wood, Longueval, Contalmaison, and many other bitter sectors of this the longest and bloodiest battle ever fought. The end result of this welter of carnage was no worth-while gain of ground. But it could be argued that the blood-bath wore down the German military machine more than that of the allies.

In the frozen winter of 1916–17 the 7th Battalion was disgruntled by the order from its General to put on the remarkable kit of gum-boots and trews instead of the kilt, so as to avoid 'trench feet' and frost-bite.

In the spring of 1917 most of the Black Watch Battalions in France took part in the first battle of Arras, and helped to take Vimy ridge, which was to become invaluable a year later. In the attack on Guémappe 70 men of the 9th Battalion held out all day, surrounded on $3\frac{1}{2}$ sides—until they were ordered to withdraw in order to straighten the line. By the end of the battle of Arras the 9th had been reduced to 130 men and two company officers. By now the Germans had withdrawn to the shorter, less vulnerable Hindenburg line. The 1st and the 4th/5th Battalions took part in the cruel third battle of Ypres in July and August. In the pill-boxes and mud-holes around Passchendaele the 4th/5th were cut down to a handful—'C' company numbered one officer and six men at the end. But it was brought up to strength again in time to fight as a Battalion in the closing stages of the battle, in that sea of choking, fetid mud, in which tanks and men and animals floundered hopelessly and perished. At the farthest point the British advanced four miles. The Germans sold every inch of ground as extortionately as Shylock. They took nearly two lives for every one of theirs.

Roll-Call of the 1st Black Watch near Bethune just before the great German offensive of 1918

In the spring of 1918 the Germans made a desperate, last chance thrust to break through the British line on the Somme, and separate them from the French. This supreme offensive was code-named 'Michael'. In part of the field the Germans outnumbered the British by four to one. In the fog of the early morning of March 21 6,000 heavy German guns thundered together on the British trenches. And 37 German divisions were launched simultaneously on a front of 40 miles against 17 British divisions. The thundering line of battle stood, and in the air Death moaned and sang. The 1st Battalion met the monstrous anger of the guns and the crunch on Givenchy ridge, which was a maze of crumbling galleries and craters.

The account of their savage underground warfare, illuminated in lurid flashes by Véry lights and flame-throwers, choked with gas, reads like one of the more ghastly circles in Dante's Inferno. B Company in Givenchy Keep started the day with two officers and 40 men; they finished with one N.C.O. and eight private soldiers; and somehow they held the little circular fort under all the tons of explosive hurled on top of it. The 4th/5th was split in two, but each half continued to fight its separate nightmare battle. They lost 25 officers and 350 men, and after the battle had to absorb the remains of the 9th Black Watch in order to retain their identity.

The 6th and 7th Battalions took the German offensive in front of Bapaume, and for five days and nights were hammered stubbornly backwards, continually outflanked and cut off. It was here that the Commanding Officers of the two Black Watch Battalions met in the same dug-out, and fired rifles together at the advancing enemy. The two Battalions virtually ceased to exist, losing between them 43 officers and 1,247 men during the pounding retreat. The gossamer British line sagged back nearly 40 miles, but somehow it held. And because it held the war was won.

In July the 6th Battalion was moved south in support of the French attack in Champagne. And at Bois de Courton, a dense wood near Rheims as impenetrable as the forest at Ticonderoga, they had more than 450 casualties. As a result the whole Battalion received the Croix de Guerre as a unit award. Only one other British Battalion has ever won this honour, which the 6th/7th wore on their sleeves from then on. The 4th/5th also fought with the French in Champagne in July. At Buzancy the French put up a stone memorial on the highest point of the hill where they found the body of the Scottish soldier who had advanced the farthest. He was a man of the 4th/5th. The monument has on it a medallion inscribed with thistles and roses, and underneath the words: 'Here the glorious thistle of Scotland will flower for ever among the roses of France'.

In August the Germans were pushed back to the Hindenberg Line, and on September 29 in dense fog the 1st Battalion helped to break through this line, the strongest entrenchment in history. All Battalions took part in the rapid pursuit into Germany. On Armistice Day the

99

4th/5th were advancing across the plain of Fontenoy where the Royal Highlanders had received their baptism of fire 173 years before.

Meanwhile, away from the Western Front, other Black Watch Battalions had been busy. In the old Highland saying, 'While the sun shines on the earth, and the waves beat on the shore, victory now as ever follows in the wake of the kilt'. It wasn't always victory, but there was certainly some hard fighting. The 2nd Battalion was pitched straight from the ice of Flanders into the oven of Iraq. On one of the warmer days they recorded a temperature of 128 degrees F. In January 1916 they sailed immediately up the Tigris to the relief of the British Mesopotamian Expedition, which was besieged by an army of five Turkish Divisions in Kut-al-Amara. After a march of 20 miles, with no time for reconnaissance, the Battalion was thrown against the Turkish trenches in the disastrous and stupid battle of Shaikh Sa'ad. The only orders they were given were that they must attack at once, and that 'the objective was the enemy's trenches, and the direction wherever the bullets were thickest'. This was not particularly helpful, since the enemy's trenches were invisible in the mirage. The Black Watch advanced to within 300 yards of the enemy lines into the bullets and shrapnel, and there they were cut to pieces. The 120 survivors lay out in the scorching sun all day, and managed to crawl back to the Start Line after dark. With masterly restraint the Battalion diary says: 'The pity was that so fine a Battalion should have been so reduced, without an opportunity of striking back'.

For six months after this battle the 2nd Battalion were amalgamated with the 1st Battalion, the Seaforth Highlanders, who had suffered as heavy losses as they had. There were various other inept and unsuccessful attempts to break the Turkish line, but eventually in April the garrison at Kut had to surrender. During the truce after the fall of Kut a Turkish officer said that he had never seen infantry like the Highlanders—'My men are good in defence, but I have not seen men who will advance repeatedly like yours over open ground under such punishment. Only real devotion to duty will make men do that.'

These were months of dust storm, disease, mirage and malaria, and night march. At last victory started to follow in the wake of the kilt, and in 1917 the 2nd Battalion were the first British troops into Baghdad, and saved the railway station from being blown up. The General gave them the big station bell as a trophy of war. At Istabulat, north of Baghdad, in April the Watch cleared the Turks with the bayonet from a strong position on the Median Wall, the oldest fortifications in the world. An artillery officer, who watched the attack without being able to give support with his guns because of the ground, wrote: 'That day the Highlanders without help won a victory that only those who saw it can realize was among the most gallant gained in the war'.

Private Melvin, an old soldier from Kirriemuir, won the V.C. His bayonet was broken. He could not fasten it onto

Imperial War Museum

The 2nd Bn. march into Beirut behind their pipes after marching 96 miles in eight days, 1918.

Black Watch before an attack in Salonika.

his rifle. So he threw away the rifle and attacked a group of Turks single-handed. With bayonet and fist he disposed of three of them. And brought back in triumph another six, who were in no mood to argue.

In 1918 the 2nd Battalion moved on to Palestine. Here, to avoid mosquito bites, they exchanged their kilts for long khaki drill trousers. In September they took part in Allenby's classic attack which finally broke the Turkish armies. At the battle of Sharon they advanced 5,000 yards through a maze of trenches in 50 minutes. This day the Highlanders captured 293 prisoners and an impressive amount of military hardware for the loss of only two men. Then they marched after the retreating Turks to Tripoli, 287 miles in a fortnight, over sand and rock, in pouring rain or furnace heat. Here the war ended for the 2nd Battalion.

The 10th Battalion spent almost the entire war in a grim and uncomfortable deadlock at Salonika. A joint British and French expedition coming to the help of the Serbians was locked fast in trenches up against the Bulgarian and Austrian armies. Philip's peerless son may have been able to carry his great war out of Macedon; but in 1916 in Macedonia the Great War was immovable, forgotten, tedious. It was unhealthy too, with temperatures high over the 100s. In one month the Black Watch had 140 raging cases of malaria, to say nothing of dysentery and sand-fly fever. It was too hot to work after 9.30 a.m. And the Highlanders were so weakened by disease that on one three-mile march with packs, a third of the Battalion had to fall out.

One of the few breaks in the monotony was, oddly enough, the trench-digging. The diggers turned up any number of exciting archaeological objects—Tanagra statuettes, beautifully carved heads, copper ornaments, and a ten-foot long tusk. The one major battle was a night attack on the Bulgarians at Lake Doiran in 1917. It was unsuccessful. It is probably true that no Division in the whole war was asked to attack, almost unsupported, so strong a position on so wide a front, as the Black Watch's Division had to take on at Doiran. The Regiment had 383 casualties, and won a Battle Honour.

In 1918, at last, the 10th Battalion was posted to France. But as soon as it arrived, it was broken up and divided among other short-handed Black Watch Battalions.

The 13th Black Watch started the war as the Scottish Horse; and the 14th as the Fife and Forfar Yeomanry. By 1916 it had been realized that this was not going to be much of a war for cavalry. And the two Yeomanry Regiments were dismounted, and transformed into Royal Highlanders. The 13th spent the war in Macedonia, before going to France to join in the final advance. The 14th spent most of the war in Palestine, fighting at Gaza, Beersheba, and Sheria. It also provided the first Christian guard over the holy places in Jerusalem after a Moslem occupation of more than seven centuries.

The Black Watch of Canada, the oldest sister Regiment of the Black Watch, had a bloody and glorious war. Like the original Independent Companies of 1725, the Royal Highlanders of Canada, raised in 1816, were composed of 'gentlemen banded together to preserve peace'. After much lobbying, two Battalions of the Royal Highlanders of Canada secured for themselves the numbers 42nd and 73rd, to match their sister Regiments. They covered themselves with glory at the sacred places of Canadian history—Vimy Ridge, Passchendaele, Regina Trench. One Battalion won itself five V.C.s. And during the first of many merry meetings with the 1st Battalion of the original Black Watch, the Canadians received the right to wear the red hackle.

Chapter 8

AFTER THAT WORLD-EARTHQUAKE, the scattered Battalions trickled back to Scotland and civilian life in dribs and drafts and drabs. They came to pipes and parades of welcome, to tramp of marching feet through Perth, and with the empty echo of feet that had not come back. The 6th Battalion came home via Paris to receive its Croix de Guerre. The Service Battalions were disbanded. Those gluttons for punishment, the Territorials, returned to week-end soldiering in their own areas.

The two regular Black Watch Battalions tried to recapture the well-ordered routine of peace-time soldiering, comfortably bounded by rifle range and route march, and by Adjutant's parade where almost as few secrets are hid as will be at the Last Judgement. But this brave new world was no longer as intelligible nor as well-ordered as it had been after all the other wars. The familiar rituals of blancoed spat and glittering mess silver had lost their magic in the mud of Flanders. Britain was terribly tired of war and of soldiers. In the well-known garrisons in India and the Sudan the Black Watch rebuilt the formal pattern of its family life. Perhaps it was an introverted life, old-fashioned, isolated from the rush of a century run mad. But it protected its members. It gave them a comprehensible frame-work in which to live. It jealously preserved the basic Black Watch virtues and skills and traditions for the day in which they might be needed again. In a shifting world there is comfort, stability, and even merit in a perfectly polished Highland brogue, and in a slow march with the pipers gliding as stately as a squadron of schooners under sail.

During these locust years there were changes which seemed important at the time. The army started to march about in threes, instead of forming the time-honoured fours. The Bren replaced the Lewis gun. In 1922 the Regiment once again made a minor readjustment in its official name. From being The Royal Highlanders (The Black Watch) it became The Black Watch (Royal Highlanders). In 1937, in its final nominal metamorphosis, it became The Black Watch (Royal Highland Regiment), reverting in the brackets to the old title given to it after Fontenoy by George II. This is still its full formal name today. Across the water Hitler was building tanks, and submarines, and the Luftwaffe.

If the army was not ready for war in 1939, that was not entirely the fault of the army. When the 1st Battalion went on manœuvres in August 1938, it had 22 Bren guns instead of 50. Its anti-tank rifles were represented by lengths of gas-piping stuck into pieces of wood. Blue flags were symbols for the carriers it did not have. It had neither mortars, nor anti-tank guns; nor even any flags to represent them. The manœuvres were watched by an interested audience of the military attachés of Germany, Italy, and Egypt. The 2nd Battalion was already on active service in a turbulent Palestine, stirred up by the Mufti of Jerusalem. Hunting the armed Arab bands, or 'Oozlebarts', who roamed and raided through the rugged country of Judaea and Samaria, was the sort of work which the Black Watch had been doing for more than two centuries, and was very good at. Life was exhilarating. A man could understand his function and his place.

When war at last erupted, strange new jobs and new modes of military thinking had to be learned in a hurry. Lenin said: 'In every Englishman's head there is a plank through which no new idea can penetrate'. In 1939 new ideas had to penetrate fast. It was a painful process. The confusion of the First World War had been a confusion of stagnation, of immobility. Battles and Battalions merged and became indistinguishable from each other over a muddy half mile. The new war was a confusion of ceaseless movement at all of the round world's imagined corners. This new mobility and incoherence of war took the red hackle on far-flung journeys, through vast jungles and idle deserts, from the steaming Irrawaddy, to the vertiginous cliffs around Cassino. The history of the Black Watch in the 1939–45 war is inevitably disjointed and breathless; war and life itself were out of joint.

In the old wars the infantry soldier had been the backbone of the battle. With his bullet and bayonet he had doggedly guarded his Colour, or his self-respect, borne the brunt, and won his Battle Honours. Now he had to learn to join in combined operations with tanks, air support, and naval guns—to say nothing of new mechanical monsters with names like 'Crocodile' and 'Wasp', spouting gulfs of liquid fire. The traditional Black Watch skills of the poacher, the burglar, the sharp-shooter, and the long distance runner were still needed. But they were not much use on their own against dive-bombers or tanks. And there was no need in this new dimension of war for the massive blocks of infantry which had held the British line from Fontenoy to the Somme. Only six Battalions of the Black Watch saw active service in the Second World War.

The foot-soldier had to learn to be mobile, on wheels as well as on legs, to co-operate as a small piece of a huge jig-saw, to take initiatives on his own. The Black Watch was to hitch-hike across North Africa on the back of tanks. It crossed the Rhine in 'Buffaloes'. It dropped on parachutes. And in the monsoon-rotting jungles of Burma, Black Watch 'Chindits', alone and unsupported, fought some of the loneliest battles in the Regiment's history. At the end of the day even in this war the infantry were still the scavengers and the kings of the battlefield, who had to move in, and tidy up, and hold the ground won by the rude mechanics. But this time they shared their battles and their old importance with the tanks and gunners and bombers. No longer did the Black Watch tilt the scales of battle on its own as at Quatre Bras or Tel-el-Kebir.

The war started badly for the Regiment, with an omen that should have shown that this was going to be different from anything that had happened before. The Highlanders were ordered to hand in their kilts, and put on battledress instead. This, said the War Office, was to prevent the Regiment being identified. 'But damn it,' protested a mortified Company Sergeant-Major, 'we *want* to be identified'. By January of 1940 there were three Battalions of Black Watch in France. And for a time not much seemed to have changed from the familiar old days of two-dimensional battle, when the infantry were pawns moved on a predictable chess-board. These were the months of phoney war, of occasional sniping, chasing smugglers, and hammering up wire entanglements which would never be used.

Then in May, out of the blue and cloudless, the storm broke. The new dimension arrived, heralded by whine of dive-bombers. This time the Germans did not repeat their mistake of 1914 of hooking their attack. Their armoured columns drove straight for the Channel ports through Belgium. The 6th Battalion of the Black Watch met the rush in Flanders, and fought a helter-skelter, somnambulant rear-guard action towards Dunkirk, across canals and rivers. They rode on borrowed bicycles, or hopped lifts on carriers. The roads were a chaos of congestion, with vehicles three abreast. But most of the Battalion came home in little groups. One Platoon marched in threes and in parade-ground step along the quay at Dunkirk, singing the song which the Regiment has sung for generations—

'You may talk o' y'r First Royals, y'r Scottish Fusiliers,
Y'r Aiberdeen Milishy, an' y'r Dundee Volunteers,
But of a' the famous regiments that's lyin' far awa,
Gae bring tae me the tartan o' the Gallant Forty-Twa.'

When the German onslaught burst, the 51st Highland
Division, which included the 1st and 4th Battalions of the
Black Watch, was down south in the Saar, sharing the
French hallucination that this was still the age of trench
warfare. They were brought round in a wide sweep south
of Paris, but too late to rejoin the main British army. The
Highlanders met the German armoured avalanche at
Abbeville on the Somme, and in six scorching, high-
summer days were hammered back 60 miles. Communica-
tions were a nightmare of confusion. Dispatch riders
roared off into the dark, and disappeared without trace.
Battalion destinations were changed at the last minute,
after a night withdrawal had already started.

On June 5 the 1st Battalion had to defend a 2½ mile

Imperial War Museum

*The Black Watch hold a position on the desperate retreat to Saint-Valéry,
1940.*

front of broken country against overwhelming numbers of German tanks. Platoons hung on until they were swamped, and then fell back to another position. At first the Highland Division had a French armoured Division under an officer called Charles de Gaulle in support. But this was soon transferred to another sagging sector. And the Highlanders were left with only their Divisional light reconnaissance tanks, hopelessly out-gunned and out-numbered. A squadron leader of these light tanks was asked by a sarcastic Black Watch Jock: 'Ca' thae things tanks? They're knockin' them oot three a penny up the road yonder'.

Eventually on June 12, on a black day for Scotland, the Division was squeezed remorselessly into the tiny, cliff-hung port of Saint-Valéry. Tanks and heavy mortars pounded them from three sides. They had no food, no water, and only what ammunition they could pick up lying abandoned. Groups of French wandering across their front with white flags hampered their shooting. The Navy's flotilla of 207 assorted vessels was stopped by fog on the crucial night from coming in to evacuate the Highlanders. When orders arrived from London to surrender to the German General, Erwin Rommel, many of the men burst into tears. Pockets of Highlanders went on fighting for six hours after the surrender, pretty well with their bare hands against tanks.

Only one officer and 18 men of the 1st Battalion escaped. The 4th Battalion however got clean away. It had been sent hastily ahead to Le Havre to prepare the defences, and make the way smooth for the rest of the Division. In the event the only thing left to evacuate was the 4th Battalion itself. It was now sent to Gibraltar as garrison. And there it missed the main stream of the rest of the war, burrowing away galleries and observation turrets in the great mole-hill.

The 2nd Battalion had also been learning bitter new

lessons about tanks and air power the hard way. It had moved from Jerusalem to British Somaliland—for the whole of the war it served under its old Subaltern, by then General, Wavell. In August 1940 this Battalion fought a fierce rear-guard action at Barkasan, alone against a heavy force of Italian and native troops and tanks. The British artillery consisted of one Bofors, and one captured Breda anti-tank gun with only five rounds. There were no machine guns. 'A' Company made an old-fashioned, yelling bayonet charge down a hill, beating hundreds of flabbergasted enemy before them. But bayonets and the bravery which had carried the Black Watch through so often before were no longer enough. Behind the screen of this battle the whole British garrison in Somaliland got away safely with only 260 casualties. Churchill sent a red-hot cable to Wavell expressing displeasure at the small number of British casualties, and hinting that this showed that the troops had not fought hard enough. The intrepid Wavell replied: 'A big butcher's bill is not necessarily evidence of good tactics,' a message which irritated the Prime Minister intensely. In fact the British killed 1,800 Italians during the withdrawal. It is hard to see what more they could have done, with no tanks, and with the enemy aircraft dominating the sky completely.

In October the 2nd Battalion was moved to Crete, and dug in around Heraklion, which has always been one of the keys to the island, ever since King Minos held his *corridas* at Knossos four miles away. The British force on Crete was again starved of equipment as it had been in Somaliland, because everything had to be sent to Greece. When it became obvious that Greece was going to fall, the material of war started to trickle in to Crete, 'too little, too late, and much of it was sunk on the way'. The garrison was left alone, without air cover, to defend the island with the traditional weapons of the British infantry. And the old weapons were no longer relevant.

Airborn invasion of Crete, 1942. The Black Watch at Heraklion shoot down a paratroop 'plane.

In May 1941, after a tremendous battering by dive-bombers, the sky was suddenly filled with puffs of thistle-down. There was a gasp of amazement, and a moment's hush along the whole Black Watch position. It was the first big parachute invasion in history. The Black Watch picked off the German paratroops as they fell, like plump pigeons. But for the next ten days more and more were dropped, prudently behind the mountains now, and out of range of Heraklion. The Battalion hung on grimly by its finger-nails, in isolated pockets unable to move by day-light, except for the piper who always played Reveille around the air-field after the dawn air-raid. At last London decided to evacuate the island. At midnight the Highlanders crept down to the beach to the cruisers wait-ing to ferry them away. They had a terrible journey to Alexandria, dive-bombed and torpedoed all the way through the narrows at the eastern end of Crete. More than 200 of the Black Watch were killed on the voyage.

A year later the Commanding Officer of the first German

parachute Battalion dropped at Heraklion was captured in Libya. He told his interrogators: 'My first surprise was when I found the position was held. The second was when I discovered who the infantry were. The battle continued with great ferocity for two days. The Black Watch never surrendered. Had it been any other Regiment, *any other*, all would have been well. Eventually we were at our wits' end. I had but 80 men left of my 800, no food, little ammunition; our food was being eaten by the Jocks.'

Next the 2nd Battalion was put into Tobruk to relieve the Australians, who had been besieged in that bull-dogged citadel for six months. The short dusty perimeter was defended by wire, mine-fields, and subterranean galleries. Dismembered vehicles and litter lay everywhere. The big German gun called 'Bardia Bill' barked and boomed over the fortress. In November the Battalion broke out of Tobruk on a sortie to link up with the Eighth Army advancing from Egypt. The plan was far more complex than the things which the Black Watch had been asked to do in old-style battles in the far-off forgotten wars. But for once the Highlanders had been given a generous ration of infantry tanks. In fact the tanks lost themselves in the flat, featureless desert, in which the only land-marks were tangles of wire. And there was plenty of wire around to confuse the issue. So the Black Watch had to go in alone with the bayonet, as they had been doing ever since Fontenoy. The pipers played the Battalion in with 'Highland Laddie', the Regimental march, and 'The Black Bear'. This last tune has a pause for a yell at intervals, and is traditionally played when a final effort is needed from tired men.

Two hours later 8 officers and 60 men were left to take the final objective out of 32 officers and 600 men who set off from the Start Line. A Gunner Major wrote after the battle: 'I class this attack of the Black Watch as one of the most outstanding examples of gallantry combined with

Dance on the deck of a wrecked German ship, North Africa, 1942.

high-class training that I have seen. Not one of us who was there will forget such supreme gallantry'. It was magnificent, but it wasn't the ideal way to wage war in 1941. After Tobruk, the 2nd Battalion was sent first to Syria, and then to Burma to meet the Japanese invasion. Rangoon fell before the convoy reached it, so they were diverted to Bombay. Here they studied new arts of jungle warfare. In their spare time they coped with a horrendous, cheek-cracking cyclone, and Congress Party agitators.

While the 2nd Battalion was learning about the new faces of war under Wavell, back in Scotland, after that Culloden of Saint-Valéry, the 51st Highland Division had sprung again from the ashes. It included the 1st, 5th, and 7th Battalions of the Black Watch; and in August 1942 the Division arrived in Suez. All three Battalions played their parts at Alamein in October. Fragments of that intricate, interlocking battle emerge from the diaries. In

Black Watch patrol probes towards Mersa Brega in Libya on the advance from Alamein to Tripoli, 1942.

between the thunderous Bedlam of the shells came the music of the pipes from one end to the other of the advancing Highland Division. Navigating officers trod warily ahead with compasses, leading the way through the lethal labyrinth of mine-field and booby-trap. In the 5th Battalion the Regimental barber had the wire-cutters— 'Get a bloody move on, Jock', shouted a voice in the dark; 'You're no cuttin' hair now'. The Highland Division punched a corridor through the deep enemy positions and minefields to let the tanks pass through into the open desert. A 19-year-old Black Watch piper was hit three times. He piped on, lying on the ground, until he died. When he was found next morning, his stiff fingers were still on the chanter. The 7th Battalion lost six navigating officers and 250 men on that first moonlit night of the 12-day battle. But for the first time the Black Watch had the weight of the new machinery and the new expertise on their side. And for the first time in the war Britain won a battle, the battle which 'hit the enemy for six' right out of Africa.

Now the Highland Division pounded in the pursuit of

Black Watch Bren gunner rides across North Africa on a tank, 1943.

Rommel over the dusty, bumpy tracks to Tripoli, through fields of evil, jack-in-the-box 'S' mines. They learned to work with tanks, to ride on tanks, to use wrecked Valentines as pill-boxes. Since Saint-Valéry they had become good at the new skills. Tripoli was captured in January, 1943. And beyond Tripoli in Tunisia all three Battalions fought at Medenine, which broke the Mareth line. After this battle, nothing could stop the Eighth Army from joining hands with the First Army from the west, in whose ranks came another Black Watch Battalion, the 6th. The days of the Axis in North Africa were trickling out like sand at the top of a run-away hour-glass. The new ideas had penetrated the plank in the head of the British. At Wadi Akarit three Black Watch Battalions fought side by side in a short, bloody but unbowed one day's battle. This was a proper infantry soldier's affair. The tanks and the wireless sets were knocked out early, and the weight of the day fell on the individual soldiers in their sections, and particularly on the runners. The 7th Battalion lost 11 officers and 180 men. On the credit side it captured 1,000 prisoners, 50 big guns, and an impressive collection of minor guns and equipment.

After the end of the African campaign, the Highland Division rehearsed for a new style of amphibious invasion, scrambling down the gangways of the vast flock of 'Ducks' which had been brought over from America. On July 10 they landed in Sicily. It was a different world from the Regiment's last great sea-borne landing at Aboukir Bay. Thump of bombing and spatter of machine-guns warned the Black Watch that they were getting near the shore. The whole night was lit up by the blaze from the Navy's new rocket ships. Only the weather had not changed. It was a black night, blowing half a gale. The ships were packed, and most people were horribly sea-sick. One Black Watch Lance-Corporal actually died from sea-sickness before he could be landed. However, apart from the traditional Black Watch weather, the landing itself went well. The Black Watch had hard battles at Vizzini and Gerbini. And by the middle of August the Germans had been swept out of Sicily. The Highland Division crossed over into Italy briefly, and then came home to prepare for the biggest amphibious invasion of all.

The 6th Battalion took the place of its sister Battalions in Italy, and fought in the crannies and eyries around Cassino. Boots were muffled in sandbags. Overhead brooded the menace of the great monastery. Life was troglodytic. In Cassino town itself, which was a flat heap of rubble partly occupied by Germans, the Black Watch learned yet another new fashion of fighting. The town was flooded and pock-marked with 40-foot craters full of water. Sections of men lived in sangars built in ruined houses. Their field of vision was restricted to a few yards. It was more like the battle of Stalingrad than anything British infantry had ever experienced before. Here Sergeant William Wilson was severely wounded. He was a descendant of a soldier in one of the original Independent Companies, and still proudly possessed his ancestor's sporran. He first joined the Black Watch in 1908, and was badly wounded with the 6th Battalion in the 1914–18 war. In 1939, when he was three months short of his 50th birthday, he re-enlisted and argued his way back into the 6th Battalion. As he was carried away from Cassino, desperately wounded by a British shell which had fallen short, he sent a message to his Commanding Officer asking to be excused for 'falling out without permission'.

In May the Black Watch helped to punch the bridgehead over the Rapido river. It was such a misty morning that the new skills were useless, and the tanks blundered blind. So the Black Watch formed up in hollow square, with the tanks in the middle, and moved forward in this traditional formation which they had not used for some years. Then they fought in the scrambling pursuits and skirmishes all the way to Rome, and on to Florence. Command of the Battalion changed seven times in July because of casualties. In September they were switched to the Adriatic coast, to attack the Gothic Line, and to get more stubborn practice at house-to-house fighting. Finally in December the 6th Battalion sailed to Athens, where they helped to clear 'ELAS', the communists, out of 'Mad Mile', the long dual carriageway which links Athens to its beaches. Here they also reverted to traditional Black Watch work, and went guerrilla-hunting, on the savage mountains of Parnassus.

Over on the other side of the world, the 2nd Battalion had become guerrillas themselves—Chindits dropped for long range penetration beyond the Chindwin. The Battalion was split into two columns, numbered, inevitably, 73 and 42. They were flown into the blind green jungle in March 1944, and for the next six months skirmished, and marched, and survived the monsoon, the steaming heat, and accidents by flood and field. It was probably the most unpleasant terrain for fighting into which the Black Watch had ever been plunged, worse even than the fever-swamps of the West Indies in the eighteenth century, or the dense jungles of Kandy. They were gnawed by starvation and disease. In one month alone 70 men died of typhus. It was a dripping world where clothes were never dry, and leeches had be stripped from bodies at night. Tracks were often waist-deep in water and mud. Leather girths rotted on the mules. A 10-mile march took four days. And once it took two days to haul their tottering half-dead bodies to the top of a four-mile pass. Most of the actions were small and untidy—the general strategy of the Chindit campaign lost direction after the death of Wingate. In May, at an ambush to cover the evacuation of 'White City', 200 Black Watch scattered 1,200 Japanese. In August the last emaciated remnants charged and captured the village of Labu with the bayonet, played in on pipes specially dropped by parachute for the occasion. They were then flown back to India to recuperate.

Thousands of miles away the 51st Highland Division had been learning new tricks for war in Europe in 1944. There were new weapons like the 'Wasp' (the flame-thrower mounted on a carrier), and new techniques for crossing rivers, for patrolling, and for making gaps in mine-fields. The 1st, 5th, and 7th Battalions of the Black

Imperial War Museum

1944. Black Watch in their carriers on the push out of the Normandy beach-head.

The pipes and drums of the 51st Highland Division return to Saint-Valéry, 1944.

Watch landed in the Normandy bridgehead on D-day and soon after. For a month of heavy hammering the three Battalions held positions around the River Orne, harassed by 'Moaning Minnies' the new multiple mortars which fired 30 screaming bombs simultaneously. All Battalions took part in the break-out from Caen, and the drive to Falaise, thundering south in armoured personnel carriers by the light of searchlights reflected off the clouds. Tanks moving on the flank of the advance fired tracer to show the general direction. And so the Highland Division came back to Saint-Valéry, more than four years after its bitter disaster, and the pipes and drums played retreat. In those four years they had become unrecognizably different creatures from the traditional Black Watch soldiers. Next they were winkling out nest after nest of Germans in Holland. Many of them got their feet wet when the enemy opened the sluices of the Rhine. In that bleak mid-winter the Black Watch Battalions were turned west to help to soak up Von Runstedt's final push in the Ardennes at Bastogne. Then they fought in the three-week battle of the Reichswald Forest, which lies on the frontier of Germany and Holland, and through the middle of which ran the Siegfried Line.

The land was a soggy, squelching morass. Movement was minimal. It was unpleasantly reminiscent of the Somme 30 years before. The 1st Battalion, advancing through the dark forest, were the first troops on to the soil of the Reich. Their Commanding Officer had started the war as a Private in the 6th Battalion. At one of the battles in the forest, a Major of the 5th was noticed walking down the middle of the street which was hissing with bullets, carrying an umbrella over his head. Presumably he had borrowed it from one of the houses. When asked why, he replied that it was raining. So it was, though nobody else had noticed. So the Major, even in this war of machines, added another episode to the long and sometimes eccentric list of Regimental nonchalance under fire— the catalogue which all Regiments lovingly preserve, and which starts in the case of the Black Watch with the fat Lieutenant-Colonel who would not lie down when shot at at Fontenoy.

Once through the Siegfried Line, the last barrier remained, the wide and winding Rhine. After days of dress rehearsal of the intricate plan on the river Maas, the Highlanders moved up to their marshalling areas on the west bank. At 9 p.m. on the night of March 22 they crossed. It was a perfect night. The pale moon gleamed on the broad silver river. On the far bank writhed the biggest artificial smoke-screen ever made. The 7th Battalion's signal that they were safely across was the first to be received back at Army Headquarters. There was some hard fighting on the far bank, not all of it in the new technological style of the twentieth century. A 19-year-old Subaltern in the 1st Battalion was given an immediate D.S.O. for charging and disposing of a German machine-gun with a spade. He couldn't use his revolver because it had been knocked out of his hand by a bullet from the machine-gun.

Three platoons of the 1st Battalion were cut off all day,

attacked by tanks, self-propelled guns, and explosives, at times driven down into a single cellar. But when they were relieved, they were still hanging on to 25 prisoners. The break-out from the Rhine was the last great battle of the war in Europe. When the end came, not with the bang of a big battle but a gradual whimper, the Black Watch Battalions were sweeping up towards Bremen and Bremerhaven, mopping up pockets of last-ditch resistance.

In the campaign of north-west Europe the hideous new art of war, which the Black Watch first saw from the receiving end at Saint-Valéry, had been polished to glittering perfection. The Highlanders had learned to co-operate in close team-work with aircraft, artillery, and armour in the complicated patterns of modern war. But the machine has not yet been invented which can in the last resort take the place of the individual infantry soldier with his boots in the mud, and his weapon in his hands.

Chapter 9

AFTER THE BELLS and the bonfires, after the euphoria of V-E Day and then V-J Day, all except the two regular Battalions of the Black Watch were disbanded, or put into what Whitehall primly describes as a state of 'suspended animation'. The great armies dispersed. The great national purpose crumbled. And, as so often before, the regular soldiers were left to find their place and their function in the anti-climax of a demob-happy world, in which everybody except them was saying an unfond farewell to the big wars. But in these turbulent post-war years of Cold War, and Iron Curtain, and dismantling of Empire, at least there was plenty to do. There was never much doubt that the infantry had a function, even if politicians changed that function with bewildering frequency. One week the Black Watch was hunting terrorists; the next, it was trying to avoid awkward incidents with the prospective nationalist Government. The Regiment did not rust unburnished in isolation and public apathy, as it had after Waterloo, and perhaps after 1918. It shone in use—in immensely sensitive new situations from Berlin to Kenya to Cyprus, where the pipe band was sometimes a potent weapon of diplomacy and riot control.

The 1st Battalion was sent on an extended and confusing tour of north-west Germany in the Army of Occupation, and ended up apparently on random roulette principles in Duisburg. The 2nd Battalion was in India, being trained in gliding and parachuting, and expecting any day to be dropped over Malaysia, or Indonesia. As usual in the army, barrack-room expectation was wrong. And the Battalion went on to Karachi, then to Peshawar. In 1947 the Highlanders were up in the north-west frontier, on 'referendum patrols', learning about internal security and riot control. When independence came to India in 1948 the 2nd Battalion was the last British unit to leave Pakistan—most suitably, since the old 73rd first tasted blood in the Indian Empire against Tippoo, and had spent 96 years' service or most of its life in India. It was one of the Regiments which built the Empire with its blood and sweat. Now it was there to bring down the curtain. Karachi was crowded with garlands and emotion to say good-bye to the British Raj, and to see the Black Watch march behind its massed pipes and drums to the ship. Mohammed Ali Jinnah, the first President, made an elegant speech of farewell to the Highlanders. Old soldier Moslems stood stiff to attention on the pavements with tears in their eyes, and saluted the Colours as they passed. As the pieces of the map coloured red shrank, infantry Battalions were now being reduced, and the 1st and 2nd Battalions of the Black Watch were amalgamated yet again at a ceremony at Duisburg in front of Lord Wavell, who was by now Colonel of the Regiment.

In 1950 the Black Watch moved to Berlin, to playing hide-and-seek in the Grunewald, to guarding Rudolf Hess and a handful of other ageing Nazi war criminals in Spandau prison, to magnificent parades in the Olympic stadium, and to training National Servicemen in the mystery and majesty of Regimental tradition. National Service was a new ingredient for a regular Battalion of the Black Watch in peace time, and, many thought, a civilizing influence in both directions. In 1952 they sailed to join the Commonwealth Division in Korea for the bitter end of that bitter war fought under the nuclear shadow. The fluid lines had at last become stabilized along ridges, and there was particularly savage fighting for the ragged peaks which overlooked the enemy on either side. For instance, White Horse Hill changed hands 23 times in this the second winter campaign of the war. The Black Watch moved up to the front line in November to relieve the United States Marines on a notorious but vital hill called the Hook, which stuck out like a sore thumb into the Communist lines. It is 30 miles north of Seoul, on a tributary of the Imjin river called the Samichon. There had been a bloody battle on the Hook a couple of weeks before the Black Watch arrived—the bunkers, the wire, the trenches were still all smashed. On the night of the relief the Chinese gave an Apéritif of what was to come by a screaming dusk charge, with gongs and whistles, which killed seven Highlanders. One Black Watch private was wounded, so he shammed dead. The Communists stripped him of his armoured vest and his weapons, shoved a grenade under him, and ran away. The Jock came to like a nervous jack-in-the-box, and hurled the grenade after them.

All through November 17 and 18 there was heavy shelling on to the brown, barren Hook. By night the sandbagged, parapeted forward platoons repaired the damage of each day in the craggy crater-field. Then in the early night of the 18th an intense creeping barrage descended upon the forward bunkers, and smashed them into ruins. 'A' Company log says: 'This lasted half an hour, and we estimated that some 4,000 assorted shell and mortar bombs arrived during that period. Before the barrage lifted the first wave of Chinese was on us'. Charging with a drugged fanaticism through their own barrage, bugle-blaring, hundreds of Chinese came swarming up the slopes of the Hook. They over-ran and completely surrounded the forward platoon. But it stood its ground and fought for nine solid hours with scarcely a moment's rest, and so gave the Black Watch counter-attacks something

125

concrete to aim at. One Chinese was carrying a British portable radio, and shouting down it in English 'Hello, One Baker'. Two Chinese took refuge in the Platoon Commander's dug-out for a surreptitious smoke. He shot them with his Sten gun. At least he thought he did, until half an hour later he lit a match and saw that they had tactfully taken the ill-aimed hint and vanished.

According to a pre-arranged plan the Company Commander called down close defensive fire and air burst from his own artillery onto his own position. The Jocks and the Chinese burrowed side by side like moles for shelter as the U.S. Marines poured howling 'ripples' of 144 rockets all over the position. The 200 yards square of the Hook received 14,000 shells and mortar bombs from both sides on that ear-shattering night.

When the guns at last lifted, the Black Watch emerged to fight among the winding, pitch-dark trenches with fist and bayonet and grenade, in a blind battle like the rat-fights of the Somme. They hurled the Chinese back down the hill. At 1.50 a.m. the Chinese came screaming up out of the night again, and drove a dent into the British position. The Black Watch counter-attacked with another Company. It was a hazardous assault, because it left the whole Battalion front wide open. But it was better than losing the Hook, and spending many lives in taking it back again. After one and a quarter hours of furious blind-man's buff fighting, the Black Watch, although still heavily outnumbered, forced the Chinese back off the hill. But they made a third attack at 4.10 a.m., and disengaged 40 minutes later, after another mauling. In the Korean War the Chinese almost invariably carried all their dead away with them after a battle. But on the morning after the battle of the Hook they had left more than a hundred friendless bodies of unburied men behind them, caught on the barbed wire like flies in webs. They carried many more away. The Black Watch lost 16 killed, 76 wounded,

126

Imperial War Museum

Korea 1952. The Hook on the morning after the battle.

and 15 captured—they won their freshest battle honour. In December the General commanding the Commonwealth Division pinned medal ribbons on nine Highlanders inside the hollow square of the Regiment, while the pipes wailed. He said: 'Wherever there is a battle, the Black Watch is usually in it, and the battle of the Hook was no exception.' It was also, possibly, the last pitched battle of the old sort that the Black Watch will ever have to fight.

In 1953 the Black Watch sailed to Kenya to hunt Mau Mau. It was posted in Company groups in the dripping jungle which covers the Aberdares like a wrinkled green rug. Patrols of Black Watch stalked the gangs in the prohibited areas of the forest with ambush and cordon and 5-day endurance patrol. They padded along tracks of fine red dust, and plunged through trackless bush. They found that the best tactic against the elusive Mau Mau was to locate a gang's hide-out by day, and to close in by night in complete silence, taking plenty of time. The patrol tried to creep right inside the terrorist camp. Then at a given signal they switched on the powerful torches attached to their weapons, and opened heavy fire. The Black Watch

127

had learned a thing or two about this sort of irregular fighting from painful lessons taught them down the centuries by assorted American colonists, Kaffirs, Boers, and Japanese. But the Mau Mau were particularly elusive and unpleasant enemies. An example of the fragmentary fighting in this untidy campaign—on Christmas Eve 1953 a small patrol of Black Watch caught up with a heavily armed gang of 20 terrorists who had just decapitated an African loyalist. The Mau Mau were guarding their impressive arsenal in a wood near Thika, a township 30 miles from Nairobi. The Black Watch patrol was too small to surround the wood, so they charged straight in. A fusillade of automatics, shot-guns, and home-made rifles killed the Company Commander, Lord Wavell, the son of the Field Marshall—he had already lost his hand in a previous campaign by treating a land-mine with characteristic scepticism. The Black Watch rushed up reinforcements, surrounded the wood, and set fire to it. At 4 a.m. on Christmas Day the gang tried to break out, and were killed or captured.

Life was never dull for the infantry in the 1950s and 1960s. There were new rifles, new wireless sets, new thinking about nuclear tactics, and always new precarious situations in countries emerging from colonialism, which could only be handled by the most discreet and disciplined infantry, and perhaps not even by them. In 1954 the 2nd Battalion, resurrected out of limbo again, flew to British Guiana to keep the peace in that political scorpion's nest. Then in 1956 the 1st Battalion went back to Berlin, the neon-glittering shop-window of the West behind the Iron Curtain, where Nato always like to show the kilt if possible. The 2nd Battalion joined them there, and the two Battalions were amalgamated, as they had been so many times before. In 1958 they came back briefly to Redford Barracks in Edinburgh, to perform in the tattoo, and to guard the Queen at Balmoral. Then, on to the terraced silver-green olive groves, the vineyards, the narrow roads, the blue skies, and the vicious intercommunal cat-and-dog fight of Cyprus. The Black Watch were back at their old job of police, the 'Watch' responsible for law and order over 600 square miles of wild, EOKA-infested country in the heart of the Troodos mountains. Detachments were posted 5,000 feet up, over the head of Battalion headquarters. Donkey trains filed up through the orange groves. Small aircraft dropped supplies. Helicopters landed on perilous mountain strips. The Highlanders had the difficult job of keeping both the peace and unobtrusively out of the way during the political ferment during the first Presidential elections, and the run-down of British forces on the island. And they had to do it all under the coldly inquisitive eye of the world's press.

Regimental life was made even more unsettled during these restless years by persistent rumours about a radical reorganization of the infantry. There were hair-raising whispers down the grapevine that old tartans, and traditions, and Regiments were going to vanish overnight in a puff of smoke from Whitehall. Recruiting for the infantry was difficult, though conspicuously never for the Black Watch. So there was a new move to rationalize the infantry into larger, more flexible units, in which the men available could be deployed and cross-posted in the direction of the greatest need. In 1961 the Black Watch Regimental Depot at Queen's Barracks, Perth, was shut down, and the Highland Regiments all moved towards sharing a centralized depot at Aberdeen. The Highland Brigade all started to wear a common, 'Large Regiment' cap badge. But though the Black Watch had to wear a badge on its bonnet for the first time, it managed to keep its red hackle. The Highland Regiments fought as jealously as any to preserve their identities in a changing army. The new infantry organization made sense administratively, so long as the baby was not thrown out with the bath-water.

Efficient administration is important, but it is not the only thing of importance.

In 1963 Black Watch pipers played at President John Kennedy's funeral in Washington. They were on a highly successful tour of the States, and had just performed before the President and Mrs. Kennedy on the lawn of the White House. After the President was killed, Mrs. Kennedy asked them to come back for the funeral.

Next the Regiment went back to the rolling Rhine, to Minden, to become the first Battalion equipped with the army's new Armoured Personnel Carrier. It was the most complicated vehicle that the Battalion had ever had to run, almost as intricate as a tank. The Black Watch Jock of history, with the kilt and the bayonet, had become fully motorized, mechanized, a skilled craftsman with small arms and wireless and motor transport, ready to operate in a nuclear setting. For the first time the Regiment was prepared not for the last war, but as far as possible for the dark and doubtful future. In 1967 the Regiment was summoned hastily back to police work, this time by the United

Black Watch territorials march past their Colonel-in-Chief, Queen Elizabeth, the Queen Mother, on a marathon route march across the Highlands.

Nations. They reinforced the United Nations troops in Cyprus to keep the Greek Cypriot National Guard and the Turkish Cypriots from each other's throats. At home the Territorial Battalions were finally and sadly disbanded. In their place the Black Watch now provided two Companies of the new Territorial Reserve, the 51st Highland Volunteers. In 1968 the 1st Battalion returned to Edinburgh as part of the Strategic Reserve, as ready as the Black Watch had ever been for whatever duties the unpredictable future might bring.

Epilogue

THE SCAVENGER through the dust-bin of history usually finds there in the debris the pattern that he sets out to look for. There are enough tattered facts and empty cans of antique evidence to fit almost any theory, or theme, or conclusion, or explanation of history he wants. That is why the search for that elusive abstraction, the Regimental spirit, is a will-o'-the-wisp business. All good Regiments think there is something unique about them. Most people who have served with them, or beside them, begin to feel a special atmosphere rubbing its back along the barrack corridors like the Regimental cat. But to put this atmosphere down in black and white is like catching quicksilver. Atmospheres change. Regiments have good and bad drafts and years. Different people smell different atmospheres. Each man must sniff out a Regiment's spirit for himself, by reading the evidence of its triumphs and disasters, and by seeing the Regiment in action. One unkind theory about Highland Regiments in general, and the Black Watch as the oldest of them, is that they are all flash and dash and flourish, with not very much dogged obstinacy in ugly situations. The Adjutant of the Royal Welch Fusiliers in Robert Graves's autobiography of the first world war, *Goodbye to All That*, put this view in its simplest and most extreme form—'The Jocks are all the same, the trousered variety and the bare-backed variety. They're dirty in trenches, they skite too much, and they charge like hell—in both directions.'

In fact the unvarnished evidence of the history of the

Black Watch points in precisely the opposite direction to this picture of the Highlanders hellishly charging in every direction. Very many of the great moments of the Royal Highland Regiment have been stubborn withdrawals covering the rest of the British army, bloody, obstinate defences, hopeless attacks when everyone else has given up. From Fontenoy and the tangled tree-trunks of Ticonderoga, to the desperate siege of Mangalore, to Corunna and Quatre Bras, to the corpse-strewn crater-fields of Loos, to Crete and the Hook, the story is of dour ferocity and stubborn steadiness. When the line falters, the typical Black Watch Jock of history grabs his bayonet and holds grimly fast.

This may be why so many Regiments around the Commonwealth have allied themselves to the Black Watch, and have borrowed its tartan and traditions. The Black Watch (Royal Highland Regiment) of Canada, the oldest sister Regiment, now has more soldiers serving than the original Black Watch itself. The New South Wales Scottish and the New Zealand Scottish are both allied to the Black Watch. So are the Transvaal Scottish, even though South Africa has left the Commonwealth. They had a heroic 1939–45 war in East Africa, Abyssinia and Tobruk—and when the war moved out of Africa very many of them volunteered to serve with British Black Watch Battalions. Southern Rhodesia sent two officers and 42 men to the 2nd Battalion in the last war. And the Tyneside Scottish, raised in 1939, were affiliated to the Black Watch. On the retreat to Dunkirk they held up enemy tanks for some hours by charging them with fixed bayonets and grenades.

One possible clue for the dedicated tracker-down of Regimental spirits may lurk in the fact that the Black Watch has always been notorious as a nest of writers, scholars, and literary men. More than 90 Black Watch men have produced chronicles of their Regiment from General David Stewart of Garth to Brigadier Sir Bernard

133

Fergusson. Stewart of Garth, one of the earliest, the chubby, spectacled, beaming eighteenth-century Royal Highlander, pinned down in words the Regimental spirit of the first men of the Black Watch better than anyone else—'In forming his military character, the Highlander was not more favoured by nature than by the social system under which he lived. Nursed in poverty, he acquired a hardihood which enabled him to sustain severe privations. As the simplicity of his life gave vigour to his body, so it fortified his mind. Possessing a frame and constitution thus hardened, he was taught to consider courage the most honourable virtue, cowardice the most disgraceful failing; to venerate and obey his chief, and devote himself for his native country and clan; and thus prepared to be a soldier, he was ready to follow wherever honour and duty called him. With such principles, and regarding any disgrace which he might bring on his clan and district as the most cruel misfortune, the Highland private soldier had a peculiar motive to exertion. . . . When in a national or district corps, he is surrounded by the companions of his youth, and the rivals of his early achievements; he feels the impulse of emulation strengthened by the consciousness that every proof which he displays, either of bravery or cowardice, will find its way to his native home.

'He thus learns to appreciate the value of a good name; and it is thus, that in a Highland Regiment, consisting of men from the same country, whose kindred and connections are mutually known, every individual feels that his conduct is the subject of observation, and that independently of his duty as one member of a systematic whole, he has a separate and individual reputation to sustain, which will be reflected on his family and district or glen.'

There is no dispute that in those early days the Highland Regiment was different from any other unit in the British army. It was different in the language it spoke, in the kit it wore, and in its unique family spirit. There is clear evidence that Highlanders enlisted in the Black Watch not for the money (8d. a day), not out of desperation, not to avoid prison, not to escape from grinding poverty or from a woman, not for the other tired and traditional reasons for which men signed on in other Regiments. Men joined the Black Watch for the love of honour, and for adventure. Down the years this difference was gradually diluted. Men did start to join the Black Watch for the time-honoured reasons—'Back to the army again, Sergeant, Back to the army again, out o' the cold an' the rain.' But there were always protests from the Regiment when drafts of less reputable men were sent to it, especially if they came from the streets of the big cities of England and Ireland.

The clannish pride of the Black Watch was certainly still strong a century ago. Sir Colin Campbell relied on the prickly racial pride of the Highlander in his stirring address to the Highland Brigade before the battle of the Alma. '. . . no soldiers must go carrying off wounded comrades. If any man does such a thing, his name shall be stuck up in his parish church'. Sir Colin knew that to threaten to disgrace a Highlander in front of his family and friends was a much more formidable deterrent than a court-martial, or other more conventional methods of military discipline.

The eyewitness account of the Black Watch Sergeant recruiting for the Napoleonic wars shows that in the early nineteenth century the most important inducement for new recruits was not the money, but the 'braw dress'. And it is probably still true that even in the purposive, abrasive twentieth century, men join the Black Watch not to become tradesmen or technologists, not because they 'get more out of life in the army' (or whatever the latest Ministry of Defence advertising slogan may say), but because of the glamour of the kilt and the pipes, and the lure of the traditions for which the kilt stands, and for which the pipes make the hairs at the back of the neck bristle. The reason Highland Regiments fight so hard to keep their tartans and the other items of dress which might seem trivial to outsiders, is that these pieces of drapery are symbols of their difference and their pride. A Corps of Infantry in battle dungarees would not have hung on so grimly at Fontenoy—and probably not at the Hook either.

The Black Watch Jock of today tends to come from the municipal housing estate rather than from the lonely glen. He is nursed in the Welfare State instead of in poverty and hardihood. Gaelic is spoken in the officers' mess only on rare ceremonial occasions. But the clan pride of the Black Watch is still handed down as a form of spiritual inheritance. The Highlands of Scotland are still separate, different from the rest of the Kingdom, preserving old-fashioned values. They gave a hint of their difference for instance in 1963, when Sir Alec Douglas Home fought his by-election in West Perthshire. A member of the B.B.C.'s late night squad of satirists stood as an independent candidate, when 'satire' was at the peak of its soaring success. In any other constituency he might have collected at least a few hundred votes. But Perthshire was not in the least amused. And the satirist polled only an insulting handful.

The Regiment retains its old values, and its old names. It is still stiff with Campbells—nearly a hundred Campbells have been regular officers in the Black Watch. And you could form a formidable platoon of officers called Colin Campbell. But even non-Campbells and non-Highlanders seem to be able to absorb something of the old clan feeling of the Regiment, without being born into the clan. There is the story of two Lancashire boys in the Black Watch who got into an argument. It ended with one of them saying, from the Everest of an infinite superiority: 'Ah've been a Jock longer than tha'.

The spirit of the Regiment which was not created by any single chieftain, but by the native love of the Highlanders for soldiering may be hard to pin down in words. But to judge from recent history the spirit still seems to work in practice. The heart is still Highland. And only a rash and reckless optimist would take a chance that the unique virtues of the Black Watch will never be needed again by Britain.

The Highland Laddie

Known by Regimental Custom as 'HEILAN' LADDIE

(Regimental Quick March)

The march is here scored for the pipes which explains the unusual notation.

138

The Black Watch

1624   Independent Companies first raised to 'watch' the Highlands.

1725   Six Independent Companies reformed, locally known as the Black Watch.

1739   Independent Companies amalgamated into The Highland Regiment of Foot.

1743-45   Flanders and Fontenoy.

1756–67   America—Battle of Ticonderoga, 2nd Battalion raised, capture of Montreal, Martinique, Havana, Battle of Bushy Run.

1767–75   Ireland.

1776–1788   American War of Independence—Brandywine and the first red hackle.

1st Battalion	*2nd Battalion, the old 73rd*
1789–95 Service at home and Flanders.	1779 2nd Battalion raised again.
1795 Capture of St. Lucia and St. Vincent.	1782–1806 India and Ceylon—siege of Mangalore, Seringapatam, Pondicherry, Mysore; redesignated 73rd Highlanders.
1795–1808 Mediterranean —Minorca, Aboukir Bay, Alexandria	
1808–1809 The Corunna and Walcheren expeditions.	1809–1815 Australia and Ceylon—capture of Kandy.
1809–1813 The Peninsula	1813 2nd Battalion, 73rd Gorde.
1813–1814 Nivelle, Nive, Orthes, Toulouse.	

1815 Quatre Bras and
Waterloo.

1816–53 Ireland, Gibral-
tar, Malta, Greece,
Scotland.

1854–55 Crimea, the
Alma.

1857–68 India—the
Mutiny, 8 V.C.s,
Cawnpore, Lucknow,
Sissaya Ghat.

1874 Ashanti War, cap-
ture of Kumasi.

1815 2nd Battalion at
Waterloo.

1816–46 Scotland, Canada
Montevideo.

1846–58 The Kaffir Wars.

1858–81 India, Hong
Kong, Ceylon.

1881	42nd and 73rd Regiments reunited as 1st and 2nd Battalions. The Black Watch.
1882–85	Egypt and Sudan—Tel-el-Kebir.
1889–1902	Boer War—Magersfontein and Paardeberg.
1914–18	The Great War—25 Battalions of Black Watch, called by Germans 'the ladies from hell'. 6th Battalion awarded Croix de Guerre. French memorial: 'Here the glorious thistle of Scotland will flower for ever among the roses of France'.
1937	2nd Battalion Palestine.
1939–45	Second World War—Black Watch serves at Saint-Valéry, Crete, Tobruk, Alamein, Sicily, Cassino, D-day, and in Burma as Chindits.
1948	2nd Battalion the last British unit out of Pakistan.
1952	Korea—Battle of The Hook.
1953	Mau Mau in Kenya.
1954	2nd Battalion in British Guiana.
1956–68	Berlin, Cyprus, Minden, Edinburgh.
1963	Black Watch pipers at President Kennedy's funeral.

ACKNOWLEDGEMENTS

THE AUTHOR and publishers are grateful to all the men of The Black Watch from General David Stewart to Bernard Fergusson who have written the story of their Regiment.

To The Black Watch Museum at Balhousie Castle, Perth, for permission to reproduce some of their blood-stirring paintings.

To Lt.-Col. C. N. M. Blair, C.M.G., O.B.E., Lt.-Col. A. K. McLeod, and especially to Colonel G. A. Rusk, D.S.O., M.C., Director of the Black Watch Museum for eagle-eyed criticism, correction, help and advice.

The publishers would also like to thank the Imperial War Museum by whose kind permission the photographs on pp. 95, 98, 101, 102, 109, 112, 114, 115, 116, 119, 120, 127 appear.

356.11

Black Watch: military history
Royal Highland Regiment (Black Watch)
military history

Regiments: infantry: British Army
356.11
355.0942

356.11

Black Watch: military history
Royal Highland Regiment (Black Watch)
                    military history

Regiments: infantry: British Army
                356.11
                355.0942